INSIGHT POCKET GUIDE

COSTA RICA

D0019049

APA PUBLICATIONS
Part of the Langenscheidt Publishing Group
L

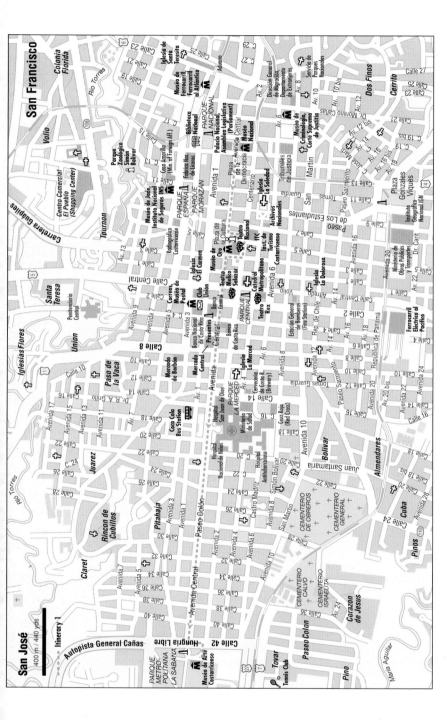

San José

400 m / 440 yds

Itinerary 1

Autopista General Cañas

Hungria Libre

PARQUE METRO-POLITANA LA SABANA

Museo de Arte Costarricense

Tovar

Tennis Club

Pino

Paseo Colón

Corazon de Jesus

Maria Aguilar

Claret

Rincon de Cubillos

Juarez

Pitahaja

Río Torres

Carretera Guadipes

Union

Iglesias Flores

Santa Teresa

Paso de la Vaca

Tournon

Volio

Colonia Florida

San Francisco

Río Torres

Parque Zoológico Simón Bolívar

Centro Comercial El Pueblo (Shopping Center)

Museo de Jade, Instituto Nacional de Seguros INS

Casa Amarillo (Min. of Foreign Aff.)

Fábrica Nacional de Licores

Biblioteca Nacional

Museo de Ferrocarril, Ferrocarril al Atlántico

Iglesia de Santa Teresita

Aduana

Radiográfico Costarricense

PARQUE ESPAÑA

PARQUE MORAZAN

Palacio Nacional, Asamblea Legislativa (Parliament)

Museo Nacional

PARQUE NACIONAL

Dirección General de Migración, Departamento de Extranjería

Servicio de Parques Nacionales

Dos Finos

Cerrito

Museo de Criminología, Corte Suprema de Justicia

Plaza de la Democracia

Tribunales de Justicia

Plaza Gonzales Viques

Instituto Geografico Nacional IGN

Iglesia El Carmen

Museo de Oro, Plaza de la Cultura

Iglesia La Soledad

Archivos Nacionales

Teatro Nacional

ITC Costarricense

Inst. de Turismo

Paseo de Los Estudiantes

Penitenciario Central

Correos, Museo de Postal

Banco Central

Club Union

Presentes

Banco Nacional de Costa Rica

Banco de Costa Rica

Teatro Melico Salazar

Catedral

Iglesia La Dolorosa

Mercado de Borbón

Mercado Central

PARQUE CENTRAL

Teatro Metropolitano Rex

PARQUE LA MERCED

Iglesia La Merced

Cerveceria de Costa R. (Brewery)

Hospital San Juan de Dios

Coca Cola Bus Station

Ministerio de Salud

Hospital Nacional de Niños

Hospital Antituberculoso

Cruz Roja (Red Cross)

Estación General de Bomberos (Fire Station)

Ministerio de Obras Públicas y Transportes

Ferrocarril Eléctrico al Pacífico

Castro Madriz

Simón Bolívar

Bolivar

Juan Santamaria

Almendares

Cuba

Pinos

San Martin

CEMENTERIO DE OBREROS

CEMENTERIO GENERAL

CEMENTERIO CALVO

CEMENTERIO ISRAELITA

Welcome

his guidebook combines the interests and enthusiasms of two of the world's best-known information providers: Insight Guides, who have set the standard for visual travel guides since 1970, and Discovery Channel, the world's premier source of non-fiction television programming.

To this end it brings you the best of the Central American country of Costa Rica in a series of tailor-made itineraries compiled by Insight's expert on the region, Dona Haber, who has been visiting the country for many years, often for months at a time. The 15 itineraries are divided into five key areas: the first five are based on San José and the Central Valley region, tours 6–8 focus on the Caribbean coast, 9 and 10 explore the Central Pacific beaches, 11–13 cover the country's south, and 14 and 15 link the highlights of the north. Each itinerary includes tips on where to eat and stay along the way, and supporting the itineraries are sections on history and culture, shopping, eating out, outdoor sports and activities, and a fact-packed travel tips section that will help you sort out the practical details of your trip. The latter section also includes advice on the best way of seeing the wildlife.

Dona Haber has been visiting Costa Rica for many years. Drawn back time after time to this beautiful country, she always finds something new as she renews her acquaintance with people and places. Though one of the smallest nations in Latin America, Costa Rica has a great deal to see and is an extremely rewarding country to visit. The cool cloud forests, idyllic beaches, majestic rainforest, steamy banana plantations and verdant pastures are all there to be explored, along with the a remarkable range of wildlife. It is a land of friendly, laid-back people, known as 'Ticos,' of pulsating music, and exotic food, and also one of the most peaceful and democratic countries in the region. The capital, San José, is a modern, bustling metropolis while historic Heredia is a colonial city surrounded by lush coffee plantations.

In this guidebook, Donna Haber helps you to sample all these different landscapes and aspects of Costa Rica, along with the simple, everyday pleasures of eating in small neighborhood cafes and buying fresh local produce at road-side stands.

Pages 2/3: Quepos port
Pages 8/9: encounter at a rodeo

History & Culture

osta Rica is a small, democratic, and peaceful country, sandwiched in the Central American isthmus between Nicaragua and Panamá. It occupies less than 52,000 sq km (20,000 sq miles), and is stunningly beautiful and diverse, perhaps more so than any other country of a comparable size. Located in the middle of a narrow strip of land known for its political and economic strife and for its wars, military figures, and dictators, the country has flourished as a peaceful democracy for more than 50 years. It was in 1949 that José (Don Pepé) Figueres established a new constitution and rid the nation of the military's overweening influence. Costa Rica has one of the highest literacy rates in the Americas, and ranks near the Western nations in terms of the standard of its health care.

When Christopher Columbus landed on Costa Rica's Caribbean coast in 1502, the country was populated by diverse peoples with distinct languages and cultures. Influenced by some of the other indigenous cultures of the Americas, the natives of Costa Rica were skilled in the arts of ceramics, gold- and metal-work, weaving, and stone-carving. Costa Rica, it seems, was the mercantile and cultural crossroads of the Americas. Columbus and his successors were particularly taken by the gold that gleamed from the Indians' armbands, collars, bracelets, beads, and bells, and by the local legends about great gold mines to the south. Today you can see golden artifacts at the pre-Columbian gold museum in San José.

The Rich Coast

Full of great expectations, Columbus named this newly discovered place the Costa Rica de Veragua (Rich Coast of Veragua). As it turned out, ironically and tragically, Costa Rica was to become the poorest and most ignored of Spain's Central American colonies. Costa Rica was not won without a struggle. Expeditions of settlers were defeated over and over again by the jungles, swamps, mountains, heat, and rain, as well as by their own bungling and feuding, and the resistance of the indigenous people. In other parts of Central America, native people lived in centralized, highly populated communities. The Spaniards conquered these communities with ease, subjugating and enslaving great numbers of Indians in the name of colony-building. The Indians of Costa Rica, however, lived in smaller, decentralized settlements dispersed throughout the country, which made their capture and enslavement more problematic.

By the time of the development of the Costa Rican colony, the Spaniards had revised some of their more brutal policies, such as *requierimento* (by which they killed Indians who refused to be baptized) and *encomienda* (enslavement of the natives). Thus the

Left: a ceremonial polychrome vessel
Right: a pre-Columbian figure

indigenous people of Costa Rica were not enslaved in large numbers by the Spaniards. But they did suffer enormous casualties as a result of their encounters with the aggressive colonists. Many succumbed to European diseases, while untold numbers fled to the mountains of Talamanca.

The first attempt, by Don Juan de Cavallón in 1561, to establish a settlement, did not meet with much success, not least due to a shortage of resources. The slave-labor force was limited, and whatever gold there had been was gone – plundered by the early conquistadors. There was little Spanish currency, and apparently no simple way to generate more. Most settler families lived on isolated farms in the Central Valley in a state of grim poverty. Their penury was such that even proper clothing was beyond their means. Dressed in simple garments made of goat hair and tree bark, they had nothing to wear to church so, despite their religious conviction, they could not even attend Sunday Mass. Cacao beans became an informal currency, and agricultural techniques learned from the locals became the Europeans' modus operandi.

Cartago, the First Settlement

Colonial communities were slowly growing in the Central Valley. In 1563 the governor of Garcimuñoz (originally near Santa Ana) moved the settlers eastward to what is known today as Cartago, where they established the first permanent Spanish settlement. The village of Cubujuqui, which later became Heredia, was founded in 1706; Villa Nueva de la Boca del Monte (today San José) in 1737; and Villa Hermosa (now Alajuela) in 1782.

Some historians point to this period as the genesis of Costa Ricans' attachment to freedom, peace, and independence. They trace the nation's democratic traditions back to those independent farmers who worked their own plots of land in the hills of the Central Valley. Even the colony's governor, so the story goes, lowered his head to the sun and dirtied his hands working his own fields. While this analysis may be based more on myth than fact, it does provide insight into the way Costa Ricans live. Today the hillsides of the Central Valley

Above: Don Juan de Cavallón
Left: indigenous inhabitants

support innumerable modest, lovingly tended houses owned by the occupants. Such home ownership by the peasantry is rare in Central America, where the disparity between poor tenants and rich landlords tends to be enormous.

Costa Ricans remained largely unaffected by the conflicts that led to Central America's struggle for independence from Spain. Indeed it was a courier on muleback who arrived with the news of Costa Rica's independence on October 13, 1821, one month after colonial officials in Guatemala had declared that country's independence from the faltering Spanish Empire. In Costa Rica this historic development was greeted with ambivalence and confusion. When the dust settled, a schoolteacher, Juan Mora Fernández, was elected the first head of state. Before long the planting of coffee trees in the Central Valley became instrumental in establishing the country's prosperity.

The Golden Bean

Coffee, the golden bean, transformed the economy of the Central Valley from bare subsistence to one of international renown. In the early years of the 19th century coffee seeds were imported to the New World from Ethiopia and Arabia. By 1840, coffee production had become Costa Rica's foremost industry and the country, with a population of only 80,000, was established as the most prosperous part of the isthmus. San José, boosted by the profits of its coffee exports, became the third city in the world to introduce public electric lighting and one of the first to enjoy the communication benefits of public telephones. Luxurious private residences, schools, banks, parks, and plazas were constructed throughout the city. The Teatro Nacional (National Theater), San José's most glorious building, was specifically built by the ruling coffee-barons as a venue for a renowned Italian diva who was touring Central America. Construction was funded by a tax on coffee.

Until 1870, the humid, swamp-infested Caribbean coast area was populated only by a few migrant fishing communities. But as the coffee trade developed, a port with access to the Atlantic was needed for the export of coffee to Europe. El Limón, a fishermen's village of five huts, was chosen. In the same year, the government signed a contract for the construction of the Atlantic railroad from San José to the new port of Limón.

Laborers from as far afield as Jamaica, Italy, and China were brought in to construct the railroad. The relentless heat and malarial swamps made for harsh working conditions. Minor Keith, the American magnate responsible for building the railroad, began cultivating bananas alongside the tracks to raise additional funds for the project. Limón thus became a port and a banana town, populated largely by Afro-Caribbean and Chinese immigrants.

Since 1872, Limón and the banana industry have experienced great booms and busts: bumper banana crops have exceeded the value of the country's

Right: coffee beans transformed the economy

coffee exports; conversely, labor problems have resulted in a number of violent strikes. On one notorious occasion of unemployment in the local industry, Keith's United Fruit Company abandoned the Caribbean Coast altogether. As for the railroad, which became known as the Jungle Train, it served communities stretching all the way from San José to Puerto Limón for 100 years. It finally closed down in 1990, due to serious financial losses and severe and continuous earthquake damage to the tracks.

In 1889 a new constitution promised presidential elections every four years. At this time Costa Rica was a prosperous, politically stable place. But as the newly generated wealth remained concentrated in the hands of a powerful elite class, the nation's politics became polarized. In response to reformist demands for greater equality, reactionaries were prepared to fight, literally, in defense of the status quo.

Joining the Allies

The reformists found their champion in Dr Rafael Ángel Calderón Guardia, who was elected president with more than 80 percent of the vote in 1939. He appeared to be just the man to lead Costa Rica into an era of social and economic reform, but he soon alienated the ruling coffee oligarchy. After the Japanese attack on Pearl Harbor, he declared war on Germany and used his emergency powers of war to confiscate the property of German families, some of whom had not only lived in Costa Rica for several generations but were connected through business and marriage to the coffee barons.

In 1942 a German submarine sank the *San Pablo*, a United Fruit Company vessel in Puerto Limón. Calderón's response was to imprison Germans and Italians in the coastal region. Anti-German riots led to the breakdown of law and order, for which José Figueres blamed Calderón. Figueres purchased air time on Radio América Latina and in mocking tones denounced Calderón and his administration. The head of the police force hauled him away in mid-sentence. Figueres spent the next two years in exile in Mexico, but he had already established a heroic reputation among many of his compatriots.

The corrupt presidential election of 1944, which elected Teodoro Picado, was the final straw for Figueres. Now advocating revolution as a means to reform Costa Rica, he set about forming alliances with other nations, stockpiling arms, and waiting for the time to strike.

Above: today Puerto Limón is a bustling center
Right: three-time president José Figueres

In 1948 Otilio Ulate, publisher of the *Diario de Costa Rica* newspaper, won the presidential election by a large margin but the *calderonista* followers of Calderón and Picado retained power in congress. Amid charges and counter charges of fraud, and ballot papers set ablaze, Ulate was arrested by Picado's police colonel, and his closest advisor, Carlos Luis Valverde, was shot dead.

The ensuing civil war consisted of a well-planned, if somewhat lucky offensive carried out by men with no military backgrounds against a president who had no heart for conflict. Figueres's National Liberation Army emerged victorious and its leader entered San José five days after the ceasefire at the head of a triumphant parade. Echoing the 19th-century English utilitarian philosopher John Stuart Mill, Figueres promised to promote the greatest good for the greatest number. In the course of his short tenure as leader of the junta, or the Second Republic as he called the new order, Figueres enacted sweeping economic and social reforms.

Abolition of the Military

Figueres's expansion of the social-security system involved legislation on child support, and low-cost health services for all. He inaugurated a minimum wage, nationalized every bank, and extended the franchise to women. Most significantly he conferred citizenship on everyone born in Costa Rica, including the Afro-Caribbeans of the coastal region, who had been treated as second-class citizens. For many, however, Figueres's most celebrated achievement was the abolition of the military. In a public ceremony, he delivered the keys of the Bella Vista military fortress to the minister of public education and, making the most of a dramatic moment, struck a sledgehammer against the wall of the fortress. Figueres argued that, if a member of the family is sick, you call in a doctor, but that does not mean that the doctor has to continue living with you for the rest of your life.

On November 9, 1949, Figueres voluntarily ceded power to Ulate. Figueres later served two terms as president, 1953–8 and 1970–74. Perhaps his most

Above: local militias featured prominently in the country's civil war

abiding legacy is the tradition of the National Liberation Party, which he founded. His successors as its leader have included in their number Oscar Arias, who, in 1987, was awarded the Nobel Peace Prize for his courageous efforts to bring peace to Central America.

Calderón's son, Rafael Ángel Calderón Fournier, served a lackluster term (1990–94) as president, and in 1994, Figueres' son, José María Figueres, was elected in his place. The young Figueres, who grappled with the country's national debt and the privatization of many of the industries once nationalized by his father, became one of Costa Rica's most unpopular leaders. The 1998 elections were won by the Partido Unidad Social Cristiana, whose leader, Miguel Ángel Rodríguez, announced his commitment to women's rights, the poor, and the young. A conservative economist, he tried to implement a tough austerity program, while awarding himself a fourfold pay rise.

In 1979 the right-wing Somoza regime in Nicaragua was overthrown by Sandinista rebels and, on the insistence of the US, to which it was financially indebted, Costa Rica became a haven for the Contras (anti-Sandinistas).

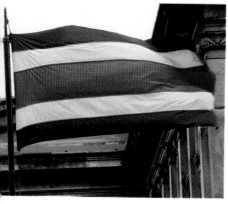

Since 1997, when the US introduced harsher immigration laws, Costa Rica's role as a refuge for Central American immigrants has become even more pronounced – it is estimated that there are 500,000 Nicaraguans in the country. Many of the 'Nicas' escaped the aftermath of the drought caused by El Niño, and the terrible damage caused by Hurricane Mitch in 1998.

Countless others were persuaded to leave by Nicaragua's abysmal economic conditions – a staggering 50 percent unemployment and a GDP (gross domestic product) that is only a sixth of Costa Rica's. Refugees also arrived from El Salvador, Honduras and Guatemala, all of which were undergoing varying levels of civil conflict. There have been inevitable problems in absorbing so many newcomers but in general the country has dealt with the situation with a typical combination of grace and tolerance.

Economic Factors

The 1980s saw a major downturn in the fortunes of the coffee and banana markets, as a result of which, by 1989 Costa Rica's national debt had reached $5 billion. President Arias negotiated millions of dollars of American aid. In recent years tourism has (along with electronics) overtaken bananas and coffee as the most important sector of the local economy. Since the mid-1980s visitor figures have risen from fewer than 400,000 to almost a million per year. The adverse effects of so many visitors on the country's biodiversity and natural beauty has been debated at length. The national park system protects about a quarter of the nation's territory, but the country is still trying to balance the competing forces of tourism and the rights of the local people and wildlife.

Above: flying the national flag

HISTORY HIGHLIGHTS

40,000–4000 BC Hunter-gatherers on the American continent drift southward, settling in small chiefdoms.

4000–1000 BC Cultivation of crops such as yucca, maize and cotton.

1000 BC–1500 AD Development of permanent agricultural communities.

1502 Columbus lands on a stretch of Atlantic Coast which he names Costa Rica de (Rich Coast of) Veragua.

1519–60 The explorations of Spanish conquistadors reach both of Costa Rica's coastlines.

1561 Juan de Cavallón establishes Garcimuñoz, Costa Rica's first community, which later becomes the city of Cartago.

1660–70 Cacao beans bring the colony its first revenue but the plantations are subject to pirate raids.

1723–82 Cubujugui (Heredia), Villa Nueva de la Boca del Monte (San José), and Villa Hermosa (Alajuela) are founded.

1821 Central American colonies win independence from Spain.

1824 The residents of Guanacaste vote to secede from Nicaragua and become part of Costa Rica.

1838 Republic of Costa Rica established.

1840s Coffee becomes big business.

1872 Work is begun on the Atlantic Railroad, linking San José with the Caribbean Coast. Bananas are planted alongside the tracks.

1880 Abolition of the death penalty.

1889 Costa Rica's liberal constitution establishes quadrennial elections.

1890 Completion of Atlantic Railroad.

1897 Inauguration of National Theater.

1934 Banana plantation workers strike against the United Fruit Company and win concessions including wage guarantees and the right to organize.

1939 Dr Rafael Angel Calderón Guardia is elected president and begins to implement social reforms.

1941 Following the attack on Pearl Harbor, Costa Rica declares war on Germany, Italy, and Japan, a day before the United States enters World War II.

1944–8 Fraudulent presidential elections keep *calderonistas* in power.

1948 The National War of Liberation is won by the forces of José (Pepé) Figueres.

1948–9 Figueres establishes a democratic constitution and institutes widespread social reforms, including the abolition of the military.

1949 Figueres voluntarily relinquishes power to the winner of the presidential election of 1948, Otilio Ulate, but later serves two further terms as president, in 1953–8, and 1970–74.

1969 Santa Rosa National Park is established.

1979 Civil war begins in neighboring Nicaragua, and Costa Rica accepts numerous refugees.

1982 Inflation reaches 90 percent as Costa Rica's economic crisis peaks.

1987 President Oscar Arias is awarded the Nobel Peace Prize for his attempts to bring peace to Central America.

1990 José (Pepé) Figueres dies. The Atlantic Railroad closes, days short of its centenary.

1990–94 Rafael Ángel Calderón Fournier, the son of Dr Rafael Ángel Calderón Guardia, serves as president of Costa Rica.

1991 An earthquake in Limón province kills 60 people and causes severe structural damage.

1994 José María Figueres, the son of José Figueres, becomes the country's youngest president at 39, and one of Costa Rica's most unpopular leaders.

1996 Swimmer Claudia Poll wins Costa Rica's first Olympic gold medal.

1998 Partido Unión Social Cristiana wins general election.

2002 Presidential election.

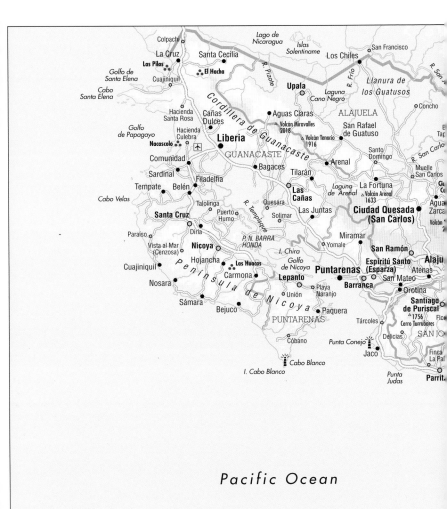

Colpachi
La Cruz
Las Pilas
Santa Cecilia
Lago de Nicaragua
Islas Solentiname
Los Chiles
San Francisco
Golfo de Santa Elena
Cuajiniquil
El Hacha
R. Pizote
Upala
R. Frío
Llanura de los Guatusos
Cabo Santa Elena
Hacienda Santa Rosa
Cañas Dulces
Volcán Miravalles 2018
Aguas Claras
Laguna Cano Negro
ALAJUELA
Concho
Golfo de Papagayo
Hacienda Culebra
Nacascolo
Liberia
GUANACASTE
Volcán Tenorio 1916
San Rafael de Guatuso
R. San Carlo
Santo Domingo
R. San Carlo
Comunidad
Sardinal
Tempate
Belén
Filadelfia
Bagaces
Tilarán
Arenal
Muelle San Carlos
Cabo Velas
Talolinga
Puerto Humo
Las Cañas
Laguna de Arenal
La Fortuna
Volcán Arenal 1633
Agua Zarca
Volcán
Santa Cruz
Diriá
Quesara
Solimar
Las Juntas
Ciudad Quesada (San Carlos)
Paraíso
Vista al Mar (Cenzosa)
Nicoya
P. N. BARRA HONDA
I. Chira
Miramar
Yomale
San Ramón
Alaju
Cuajiniquil
Hojancha
Las Huacas
Carmona
Golfo de Nicoya
Lepanto
Puntarenas
Espíritu Santo (Esparza)
San Mateo
Atenas
Barranca
Orotina
Nosara
Unión
Playa Naranjo
Santiago de Puriscal
Sámara
Bejuco
Paquera
Tárcoles
1756 Cerro Turrubares
Flo
SAN JO
PUNTARENAS
Cóbano
Punta Conejo
Delicias
Finca La Pal
Jaco
Cabo Blanco
I. Cabo Blanco
Punta Judas
Parrit

Cordillera de Guanacaste

Peninsula de Nicoya

R. Tempisque

Pacific Ocean

Isla del Coco

8 km / 5 miles

Punta Agujas
I. Manuelita
Cabo Barreto
Cerro Yglesias 634
Cabo Atrevida
Cabo Lionel
Cabo Dampier

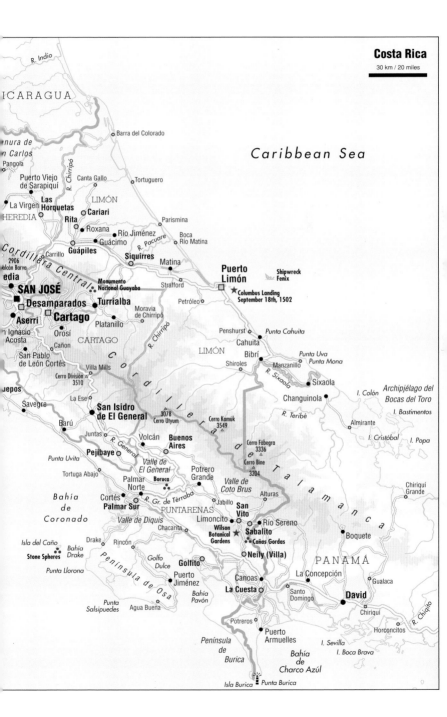

Costa Rica

30 km / 20 miles

ICARAGUA

Caribbean Sea

R. Indio

Barra del Colorado

nura de
n Carlos

Pangola

Puerto Viejo
de Sarapiquí

Canta Gallo

Tortuguero

La Virgen

Las
Horquetas

LIMÓN

HEREDIA

Cariari

Parismina

Rita

Roxana

Río Jiménez

Boca
Río Matina

Carrillo

Guácimo

Guápiles

Siquirres

Matina

Strafford

**Puerto
Limón**

Shipwreck
Fenix

edia

SAN JOSÉ

Monumento
Nacional Guayabo

Columbus Landing
September 18th, 1502

olcán Barva
2906

Desamparados

Turrialba

Moravia
de Chirripó

Petróleo

Aserrí

Cartago

Platanillo

Penshurst

Punta Cahuita

n Ignacio
Acosta

Orosí

Cañon

CARTAGO

Cahuita

LIMÓN

Bibrí

Punta Uva
Punta Mona

San Pablo
de León Cortés

Villa Mills

Shiroles

Manzanillo

epos

Cerro División
3510

Sixaola

I. Colón

*Archipiélago del
Bocas del Toro*

Savegre

La Ese

San Isidro
de El General

3078
Cerro Utyum

Cerro Kamúk
3549

Changuinola

R. Teribé

I. Bastimentos

Almirante

I. Cristóbal

I. Popa

Barú

Juntas

Volcán

**Buenos
Aires**

Cerro Fábrega
3336

Pejibaye

Punta Uvita

*Valle de
El General*

Cerro Bine
3204

Tortuga Abajo

Palmar
Norte

Boruca

Potrero
Grande

*Valle de
Coto Brus*

Chiriquí
Grande

*Bahía
de
Coronado*

Cortés

Palmar Sur

R. Gr. de Térraba

Jabillo

Alturas

San
Vito

Valle de Diquis

PUNTARENAS

Limoncito

Río Sereno

Isla del Caño

Stone Spheres

*Bahía
Drake*

Drake

Rincón

Chacarita

Wilson
Botanical
Gardens

Sabalito

Cañas Gordas

Boquete

PANAMÁ

Punta Llorona

Golfo
Dulce

Golfito

Neily (Villa)

La Concepción

Gualaca

Península de Osa

Puerto
Jiménez

Canoas

Santo
Domingo

David

Punta
Salsipuedes

Agua Buena

*Bahía
Pavón*

La Cuesta

Chiriquí

R. Chiquito

Horconcitos

Potreros

*Península
de
Burica*

Puerto
Armuelles

I. Sevilla

*Bahía
de
Charco Azúl*

I. Boca Brava

Isla Burica

Punta Burica

Cordillera Central

Cordillera de Talamanca

R. Chirripó

R. Pacuare

R. Chirripó

R. General

R. Sixaola

The
Central Valley

The sheer diversity of Costa Rica's topography gives the impression of a country far larger than this small Central American territory. There are four major mountain ranges, and innumerable rivers and waterways. The land, which rises from sea level to 3,800 meters (12,500ft), stretches from 220km (135 miles) of Caribbean coastline to 1,100 km (630 miles) of seashore on the Pacific coast. Yet the country's landmass of 52,000 sq km (20,000 sq miles) is about the size of the state of West Virginia.

The country can be easily divided into the following regions: the Central Valley, the Caribbean (Atlantic) coastline, the more developed central Pacific coast, the remote southern zone, and the lush northern region.

The Central Valley *(Valle Central)*, or Central Plateau *(Meseta Central)* as it is frequently called, is the heart of Costa Rica. Two major mountain ranges meet here in an area of only 24km (15 miles) by 64km (40 miles) that is characterized by rich, green volcanic hills and river-filled valleys presided over by three volcanoes and an expansive skyline. The people tend to be friendly, dignified, and independent. Some 60 percent of the population lives in the Central Valley – in the congested capital of San José, the major cities of Alajuela, Cartago, and Heredia, and in the myriad mountain villages and small towns that are scattered through these verdant highlands.

Sweetly Scented Air

The seat of government, the agricultural and commercial centers, coffee farms, churches, theaters, art galleries, casinos, restaurants, and universities are all concentrated in this 960-sq-km (600-sq-mile) area. The land rises from 800 meters (2,600ft) to 1,500 meters (4,900ft), and a wonderful climate features temperatures that are usually around 25°C (in the mid-70s°F). The air in the varied, beautiful countryside is soft and sweetly scented.

The following itineraries suggest ways to organize trips into the lush hills of the Central Valley, taking in coffee plantations, colonial towns and churches, orchid gardens, volcanoes (both active and dormant), and national parks. There are opportunities for whitewater rafting on the Pacuare River, and to experience the cosmopolitan delights of San José before heading off to explore the country's more remote regions.

To help you to navigate your way around, there are tips on renting a car, hiring a bilingual driver ,and reserving a tour through one of the many excellent local operators. Taxis provide a good, inexpensive way to travel, and buses go every-where *(see Practical Information, page 79).*

Left and **Right:** waterfalls and often-active volcanoes are dramatic features of the Central Valley region

1. DOWNTOWN SAN JOSÉ *(see map, p4)*

This one-day itinerary is best done on the weekend, preferably on a Sunday. Visit the National Museum, lunch in the coffee shop of the historic National Theater and check out the pre-Columbian Gold Museum. Relax on a Gran Hotel veranda, explore the National Art Museum, and take a late-afternoon stroll in La Sabana Park.

As is the case in any foreign place, it is a good idea to familiarize yourself with the city (best done with the map that accompanies this book) before you head for the streets. San José is organized on a grid system of numbered streets *(calles)* and avenues *(avenidas)*. *Calles* run north to south, *avenidas* east to west. Southern and western streets and avenues have even numbers, northern and eastern streets and avenues odd numbers.

Buildings are not numbered and, for the most part, only in downtown San José do streets have names. Hence the address of the Catedrál Metropolitana (Metropolitan Cathedral) is Calle Central, Ave 2–4, which means that the cathedral is on Calle Central between *avenidas* 2 and 4. But it is more common to give addresses in terms of distance in meters *(metros)* north, south, east, or west from landmarks, some of which, confusingly, no longer exist. Even the locals perpetually stop one another on the street to ask for directions. They seem to enjoy the interaction, and are almost always helpful. Even if you don't speak Spanish, you can generally get a friendly pointer.

Though Costa Rica is, in general, a safe country, theft is a growing problem, especially in San José. The best way to have a hassle-free day is to travel light. Carry a copy of the front pages of your passport and only as much cash as you will need. Use a money belt and leave your wallet or purse, as well as your backpack and valuables at the hotel. Ask the hotel to call a taxi for you or, if you are feeling more adventurous, ask how to get a bus to the Museo Nacional.

National Museum

The **Museo Nacional** (National Museum; Tues–Sat, 8.30am– 4.30pm, Sun and holidays, 9am–4.30pm; tel: 221-0295; admission charge) is on Calle

17, between Avenida 2 and Avenida Central. This is the former Bella Vista fortress where, in 1949, José Figueres announced the abolition of the military and dealt a symbolic blow to the wall with a sledgehammer. The bullet holes in the walls date from the civil war. The museum has a notable collection of pre-Columbian ceramics, and interesting items from the colonial eras.

As you leave the museum, turn left on Calle 17, walk half a block and turn left again on Avenida Central. Head west to the Plaza de la Democracia (Democracy Square), just below the

Left: San José. **Above Right:** Museo Nacional. **Right:** Teatro Nacional ceiling

museum. You may want to browse through the stands of the open-air artisans' market in the plaza. Then continue on foot along Avenida Central for five more blocks and you will find yourself in the middle of the pedestrian walkway, standing near a fountain. The entrance to the **Teatro Nacional** (National Theater) is one block over, on Avenida 2. The coffee shop here, a cool and quiet oasis, is ideal for lunch. The desserts are especially good.

Theater fit for a Diva

After lunch, take a stroll around the theater (tours daily; admission charge), which has an interesting history. In 1894 it was hoped that the world-renowned diva Adelina Patti would perform in Costa Rica while on tour in Central America, but she refused on the grounds that there was no appropriate venue. So a coffee tax was imposed to finance the construction of the Teatro Nacional, which was completed in 1897 and inaugurated with a performance of Gounod's *Faust*. Modeled on Paris's grand Opera Garnier, it has an opulent red velvet and gold interior. If you want to see a show here, check the program of upcoming productions on your way out of the theater.

For an understanding of the gold fever that consumed Columbus and the conquistadors visit the nearby **Museo de Oro** (Gold Museum; Tues–Sun, 10am–4.30pm; admission charge). to get there, turn right as you exit the Teatro Nacional, and walk through the **Plaza de la Cultura** (Cultural Square) and down the steps to the museum entrance. The museum's dazzling 1,600-piece collection of gold items made by Costa Rica's pre-Columbian Indians is well worth seeing.

If you feel like a rest at this point, return to the Plaza de la Cultura, head for the **Gran Hotel** and find a table on the veranda where you can relax with a drink, soak up the sunshine, and watch the Central American world go by.

If it is a weekday you can explore the **Museo de Jade** (Jade Museum; Mon–Fri 8.30am–4pm; admission charge), just a short stroll away on the 11th floor of the National Insurance Institute (Avda 7, Calles 9–11), which is home to the world's largest American jade collection, most of which dates from pre-Columbian times. There are great views of the city from here.

At this stage you might want to take a taxi back to your hotel, in which case make sure that it has a meter *(maría)*, and that the driver uses it. Alternatively, if you still have plenty of energy to burn and it's not too late in the day, head for the Museo de Arte Costarricense (Museum of Costa Rican Art), which is a 10-minute taxi ride from the Gran Hotel. Or you might opt for a walk in La Sabana Park, next to the museum.

The **Museo de Arte Costarricense** (Museum of Costa Rican Art; Tues–Sun, 10am– 4pm, admission charge; tel: 222-7155) features a large collection of Costa Rican art from the pre-Columbian period through to modern times. On the terrace, the museum's Café Ruiseñor is a good place for desserts and coffee. The museum building was once Costa Rica's airport terminal, and the surrounding park provided its runways. **La Sabana** is a large metropolitan park with tree-lined paths, a small lake, tennis and basketball courts, and a swimming pool. It is invariably packed with *Ticos* (Costa Ricans) on Sundays and is a pleasant place to walk and people-watch. If you're thirsty, buy *una pipa* (a 'drinking coconut') from a vendor on the west side of the park. When you're ready to return to your hotel, La Sabena is a good place from which to catch a taxi. Be sure to leave the park before dusk falls, as it can be dangerous at night.

Night Options

For a taste of some typical Costa Rican fare on your first night in San José, you could try La Cocina de Leña restaurant in the El Pueblo commercial center, which is the home of numerous bars and restaurants. Another recommended option is to reserve a table at El Chicote steakhouse on the north side of La Sabena park (tel: 232-0936).

To finish off the day, check out one of the city's excellent bars or clubs, where salsa and merengue are very popular. For live-entertainment listings consult the *Tico Times* or *La Nacion* newspapers. Recommended nightclub choices include La Esmeralda (Avenida 2, Calles 5–7; Mon–Sat 11am–5am) which is a great place for mariachi music, and El Cuartel de la Boca del Monte (Avenida 1, Calles 21–23), which has long been a favorite haunt of young *Ticos* and often has live music.

Above: artifact at the Museo de Oro
Right: at the Plaza de la Cultura

the central valley

2. HEREDIA – COFFEE COUNTRY *(see map, p26)*

An early morning walk in the cool hills and cloud forests above the city. Join Café Britt's coffee tour, followed by lunch at a local restaurant. Visit the town of Barva, ending the day in the historic Central Plaza.

Make arrangements in advance. Hire a driver, and reserve a place on Café Britt's 11am tour (tel: 260-2748; fax: 260-1456; info@cafebritt.com). There is also a 9am tour (year round), and a 3pm tour (Sept 15–Apr 30). Take a sun-hat, umbrella, and sweater, and wear walking shoes.

Heredia, one of the nation's oldest, wealthiest, and most historic cities, is a bustling commercial center, and the home of the National University. In the mountains above the surrounding *cafetales* (coffee plantations), the climate is cool and fresh, the landscape beautiful and green.

One of four main Central Valley cities dating from the colonial period, Heredia was founded in 1706, originally as Cubujuqui. Heredia and Cartago, the country's first capital, were conservative cities aligned with the Catholic Church and the Spanish. (San José by contrast was founded by renegade settlers banished from Cartago for defying smuggling laws; Alajuela was a free-wheeling agricultural center, where tobacco smuggling flourished.) After Costa Rica was granted independence from Spain in 1821, there was a movement in conservative Cartago and Heredia to join the Mexican Empire. The leaders of San José and Alajuela, however, wanted independent statehood. The issue was eventually decided when armies from the assorted rival cities clashed just outside Cartago. The skirmish left 20 men dead, and the liberal forces victorious. As it happened, events to the north had already overtaken the combatants: the Mexican Empire, under the leadership of Augustine I, had fallen several days prior to the battle.

National Park

The day's itinerary begins with an early-morning walk in Hotel Chalet Tirol's cloudforest reserve on the border of **Parque Nacional Braulio Carrillo** (Braulio Carrillo National Park). Leaving your hotel at about 8am, head

Above: Heredia coffee plantation

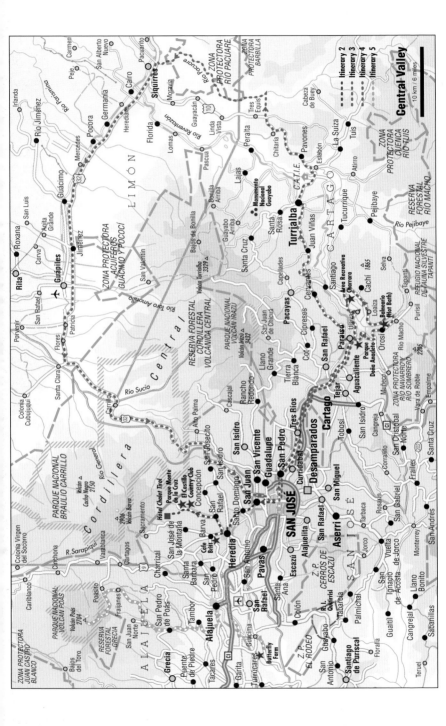

north of San José to pick up Highway 5, where it converges with Calle Central. Continue on Highway 5 through San Juan de Tibás and Santo Domingo, through the east side of Heredia, and up to San Rafael, where you should make a right turn uphill at the church. Follow this road for about 5km (3 miles), turn left at the fork and follow signs to Hotel Chalet Tirol. Tell the guard at the gatehouse that you are going to the hotel, then drive through a residential area and cypress forest to the hotel, where there are several well-maintained paths to follow. The one that leads to a dozen small waterfalls *(cascadas)* is particularly attractive. Afterward, you might stop at Tirol's lovely French restaurant for a cup of coffee or hot chocolate.

Leaving Tirol by 10.30am, allow at least half an hour to find Café Britt's HQ: retrace your path back to San Rafael and continue down the hill to the center of Heredia, where signs point to **Café Britt's coffee tour**. The tour is full of aromatic surprises, information about coffee, and lots of laughs.

For some *comida típica* (traditional Costa Rican food) at a folksy eatery, Añoranzas (Wed–Mon; tel: 267-7406) is the place. It is located on your left as you go up the hill – look out for the sign. Just up the hill, on the right, Soda La Casita also serves good *comida típica*. Another good lunch option is Los Peroles Pollo del Monte, which serves delicious juicy wood-broiled chicken.

Colonial Barva

After sating your appetite, drive down the hill toward San Rafael, and follow the signs to **Barva**. Founded in 1561, this colonial town (pop: 65,000) is one of the nation's oldest. Stroll around the central plaza, where the church and adobe houses have been restored. From the steps of the church, there is a wonderful view of the town and the mountains beyond. Also of interest are the **basílica**, the **fort** *(fortín)*, and the **Casa de Cultura**. 'Guards' frequently patrol the streets to protect cars from theft. A nod from you will indicate that you want your vehicle guarded. Tip 100–200 *colones* on your return.

Opposite the old church, on the south side, is a Pop's ice cream shop. Try one of their delicious *nieves* (fruit ices) or a *helado* (ice cream). The plaza is an excellent place for people-watching and a good spot to sit and enjoy your ice cream. Just a few blocks from the plaza, on Calle 3 between Avenidas 2 and 4, you will find Chocolates Christina, where you can purchase handmade Dutch chocolates from the Dutch expats who make them. You might like to buy a few for your return trip.

Above: Café Britt tour bus takes a break
Right: ice cream raises smiles all round

3. TURRIALBA AND THE RÍO PACUARE *(see map, p26)*

An exhilarating day of rafting. Early morning pick-up from your hotel and transportation to the banks of the Río Pacuare. Enjoy a traditional Costa Rican breakfast overlooking the Orosi Valley, and a picnic lunch on the shore of the Pacuare, returning to your hotel at dusk.

You will need to book this itinerary in advance (see below for options). Take a swimsuit, and a pair of shorts, a shirt, and sandals or tennis shoes that you don't mind getting wet, plus a towel and a change of clothes for the trip home. You will probably not fall into the river, but you will be splashed.

Costa Rica is one of the world's great destinations for rafters. It is said that the country has more accessible whitewater rivers and rapids than anywhere else. Despite its perilous appearance, rafting is a relatively safe sport. You will receive instruction from an experienced, English-speaking river guide – who also pilots your raft – and will be fully equipped with life-jackets and helmets. The rafts, which seat six people, are accompanied by a 'safety kayaker,' who can assist if anyone should fall overboard.

Many companies run rafting trips on either the Río Reventazón (which, unfortunately, is quite polluted) or the Río Pacuare. All of them will arrange a pick-up from your hotel and take you to the starting point of the rafting trip, usually stopping for breakfast on the way. Among recommended companies are: Costa Rica Expeditions (tel: 222-0333; fax: 257-1665) and Ríos Tropicales (tel: 233-6455). The itinerary outlined here is run by Costa Sol (tel: 293-2150; fax: 293-2155), which operates rafting trips throughout the year – rain or shine – on the Río Pacuare. Reservations should be made as far ahead as possible, although the company does try to accommodate people who arrive on the spur of the moment. Costa Sol's Pacuare rafting trip is pricey but it includes complete transportation, breakfast, and lunch.

Ideal for Novices

This itinerary heads east of San José, past the whitewater capital of Turrialba, and involves rafting all the way down a 36-km (18-mile) stretch of the beautiful Pacuare River, which is well-suited to novice paddlers. There are roiling patches of white water, but also long calm expanses that are ideal for leisurely paddling and taking in a panorama of canyon, waterfalls, rolling fields of coffee, sugar cane, wild grasses, and abundant birdlife. Your guide will

point out the herons, egrets, kingfishers, orioles, and other birds that live by the river. You may be fortunate enough to see a rare, iridescent-blue morpho butterfly, or perhaps a toucan or a tree sloth.

Costa Sol's minibus will pick you up at about 6.30am and take you through downtown San José to **Cartago**. Under its original name, Garcimuñoz, Cartago was established in 1561. Numerous earthquakes, floods, and eruptions of the nearby **Volcán Irazú** (Irazú Volcano) have destroyed much of its historical architecture, however, and little evidence remains of the colonial past. On your way through the

Left: look out for the elusive tree sloth

city you will see **Las Ruinas**, the ruins of a parish church that was leveled by an earthquake in 1910, as were many of its predecessors, including the original, 1570 building. You will also pass Costa Rica's religious center, the grand **Basílica de Nuestra Señora de los Ángeles** (Our Lady of the Angels), which was built to house a statue of a black virgin (La Negrita) that miraculously appeared on the site where the basilica now stands.

On the east side of Cartago is the settlement of **Paraíso de Cartago**, so named by Spaniards who found its cool weather and absence of malarial mosquitoes quite heavenly. From here it is a short distance to the Sanchiri Mirador and Lodge for a breakfast of fresh fruit and juice, *gallo pinto* (black beans and rice), scrambled eggs, bread and butter, and Costa Rican *café con leche* (coffee with milk). Sanchiri's dining area overlooks the Orosi Valley. Bright green coffee plants cover the hillsides, and the Río Reventazón, tamed by the Cachí hydroelectric dam upriver, flows quietly along the floor of the valley. An odd, triangular house, built by the American actor, Michael Landon, stands nearby.

From the Sanchiri Lodge, it is a drive of some 1¾ hours through beautiful mountain scenery, past the sugar-cane fields of Juan Viñas and the farming town and whitewater center of Turrialba, to the landing site on the Pacuare. Here you get kitted out for the rafting trip. After instruction from your guide, it is into the raft.

Hitting the Rapids

After two hours of paddling through exciting rapids and calm water, you will break for a picnic lunch on the riverbank. After lunch and a short rest, you return to the raft and continue for another two hours, past (or through) stunning waterfalls, more roiling rapids, and calm, clear water. A pass through a deep river canyon marks the end of the trip. Just outside the town of Siquirres, the raft is brought ashore at a restaurant where you can change into warm, dry clothes and enjoy a cold drink and a snack before driving back to San José.

The route back to San José picks up the Caribbean Coast Highway and takes you past Guacimo, through the Braulio Carrillo National Park and over the continental divide at Zurquí Tunnel. You should arrive back at your hotel at dusk, or just after dark.

Top: Las Ruinas are all that is left of a church repeatedly hit by earthquakes
Right: Volcán Irazú

4. OROSI VALLEY *(see map, p26)*

A day-trip to the town of Orosi, visiting Jardines Lankester (Lankester Gardens) and lunching at a delightful former coffee hacienda. See the ruins of Ujarrás and the Basílica de Nuestra Señora de los Ángeles.

Rent a car or book the knowledgeable driver Carlos Mora (tel: 232-9870 or 384-4576). Try to leave by 8am. Take a camera, a warm sweater or jacket, and an umbrella. You may need mosquito repellent at Lankester Gardens.

The Orosi Valley is simply enchanting. Fertile, dark green hills rise up from the floor of the valley where swirls of mist play with the sunlight, creating a luminous glow. Much of Costa Rica's colonial history took place in the Orosi Valley and around Cartago, and many stories of miraculous events are interwoven with historical fact.

Jardines Lankester should be visited early because it frequently rains later in the day. To get there, follow Avenida Central east through San José and the suburbs of San Pedro and Curridabat to the *autopista*. Continue through Cartago. Two blocks after the large Basílica de Nuestra Señora de los Ángeles, turn right then left onto the road leading to Paraíso; you can visit the basilica on your return. Before you arrive in Paraíso you will see, on the right, a large sign with an orchid, indicating the road to Lankester Gardens.

Orchids Galore

Jardines Lankester (daily 8.30am–3.30pm; admission charge for foreign visitors) was founded by an English botanist, Charles Lankester, who came to Costa Rica to pursue what turned out to be a failed coffee venture. Lankester bought 15 hectares (37 acres) of land to preserve local plants, especially orchids and bromeliads. Today the gardens are under the jurisdiction of the University of Costa Rica, and they feature approximately 800 species of orchid, which are best seen from February through April, when the largest number are in bloom. There are always some orchids in bloom – the gardens feature impressive displays of bromeliads, succulents, palms, and bamboo.

When you are ready for a snack, and an astonishing view of the Orosi Valley, follow the road through Paraíso, turning right at the park. The road narrows and descends into the valley. Watch for signs pointing to the turnoff

for Sanchiri Lodge, a hospitable establishment run by a Costa Rican family that has owned the land for five generations *(see Itinerary 3, page 29)*. *Café con leche* is served in tthe traditional way, and snacks include *tortilla con queso* (a large tortilla with cheese mixed into the dough), or a bowl of *sopa pozol* (a tasty fresh corn soup).

Return to the main road and continue to the town of **Orosi**. Once you arrive on the valley floor, you will see the town's colonial church, built in 1743. Inside, there is a beautiful carved altar and oil paintings of the Stations of the Cross and the Virgin of

Left: tropical vegetation. **Above Right:** the Orosi Valley. **Right:** church ruins at Ujarrás

Guadalupe. Next door is a small museum with artifacts of colonial religious history.

The surrounding hills are covered with coffee plants. If it is December or January (the coffee harvesting months) you might see coffee pickers at work. When it comes to lunch, try La Casona del Cafetal, a restaurant set in the midst of a coffee plantation (just off the road to the east of Orosi). You will see signs advertising it on your way out of Orosi. On a sunny day, it is very pleasant to sit on the veranda of La Casona, overlooking Lake Cachí.

After lunch, continue on the road heading eastward. Soon after the Cachí dam, take the left-hand turnoff for Ujarrás. Along the way, you will see plants that resemble grapevines on stakes. These are *chayote* (a form of squash). At **Ujarrás**, which has a lovely setting, you can see the ruins of a 17th-century church dedicated to the **Virgen del Rescate de Ujarrás**, which was built to commemorate the retreat, in 1666, of a group of pirates led by the notorious Henry Morgan. The pirates had appeared to be hell-bent on sacking the country and advanced as far inland as Turrialba before suddenly and mysteriously turning tail. Some say they were tricked by the Spanish governor, Juan Lopez de la Flor, who led them to fear an imminent ambush.

Basilica of the Dark-skinned Virgin

From Ujarrás, head back to Paraíso. If you are in need of refreshments, El Continentál, on the left just before you reach Cartago, is a good place to stop. El Continentál serves snacks, a variety of fruit drinks, and a delicious local *casado* dish of beans and rice, listed on the menu as a Plato Típico.

Cartago's impressive **Basílica de Nuestra Señora de los Ángeles** (Basilica of Our Lady of the Angels) is next on the itinerary. The basilica was

the central valley

built to honor a statue of the dark-skinned virgin (La Negrita) that was discovered in 1635 by a young girl walking through the forest, where the basilica now stands. Whenever it was moved from the rock, the statue would miraculously keep returning there. In 1926, the basilica was built to give La Negrita a permanent home.

La Negrita is credited with performing innumerable miracles. To look at the evidence, take a look inside the shrine room, to the left of the basilica's altar, where there are cases packed with offerings and charms from grateful petitioners whose supplications the virgin answered. Downstairs, the walls of the basilica enclose the rock where the statue first appeared. On top of the rock is a replica of the Virgin contained in a dazzling gold case. The water from a stream running under the rock is also said to have miraculous powers, and containers of the holy water are on sale at a shed to the rear. On the other side of the street a shop sells an assortment of tiny metal charms and religious items. On the return drive, follow the Interamerican Highway from Cartago back to San José.

5. PARQUE NACIONAL VOLCAN POAS *(see map, p26)*

Drive through mountain scenery to the Poás Volcano national park. View active volcanoes from a lookout point above the crater and follow trails through a landscape of wild flowers, mosses, bromeliads, and ferns. Take lunch at a local restaurant, then visit a butterfly farm.

Make transportation arrangements as far ahead as possible. Book a rental car or a private chauffeur (see page 79).The average temperature on Poás is around 50°F (10°C), so bring a warm jacket or sweater, and pack waterproof gear. An English-Spanish dictionary would be useful.

This itinerary takes you above the city of Alajuela, high into the mountains of the Central Valley, past lots of strawberry farms, nurseries, and coffee plantations, to Poás, one of the world's most accessible active volcanoes.

Try to get an early start, before 8am, if possible, because Poás becomes increasingly crowded, cloudy, misty, and cold as the morning wears on. Bear in mind too that from May through November, there is a good chance of afternoon rain.

Take the Cañas Highway toward Alajuela. After the toll booth (80 colones), continue for about five minutes to the intersection at the end of the airport runway. Turn right here, at the Hampton Inn, then immediately left, toward Alajuela. Continue on this road to Poás via San Pedro de Poás and Poasito. If you get lost, ask anyone *'¿El camino a Poás?'* for directions. On your way through **Alajuela**, you will pass the Central Park and the small but interesting **Museo Juan Santamaría** (Juan Santamaría Museum). Alajuela

Above: miraculous waters at the Basilica of our Lady of the Angels

was the birthplace of Juan Santamaría, Costa Rica's national hero. In 1856, Santamaría lost his life while setting fire to the town of Rivas in Nicaragua, the stronghold of William Walker, a notorious North American mercenary, slave trader, and self-proclaimed dictator of the country. Only in 1857, after he had invaded Guanacaste, were Walker and his men defeated by a coalition of Central American forces at the second battle of Rivas.

Bubbling Sulfur

Stay on the same road until you reach Fraijanes Lake and Chubascos. About 1.5km (1 mile) past Chubascos, you will connect with the road to **San Pedro de Poás**, which leads to the **Parque Nacional Volcán Poás** (admission charge). Inside the park, a footpath leads to the lookouts over a main crater that is about 1.5km (1 mile) wide and 300 meters (1,000ft) deep. The lake at the bottom of the crater changes color according to the volcanic activity at the time. If the water level is low you might see bubbling pools of molten sulfur.

Poás has erupted 20 times since 1834. The most notable of these eruptions occurred in 1888, 1904, 1905, 1910, and 1952–54. Poás has also produced toxic vapors and acid rain – one day in 1994, 400 visitors were evacuated from the park due to vapors of sulfuric acid. Today park officials watch the emissions level, and can close the park if they become unhealthy. To be on the safe side, you should spend no more than 20 minutes overlooking the crater.

Above: statue of Juan Santamaría
Right: Parque Nacional Volcán Poás crater

If you feel like undertaking a 30-minute uphill hike after viewing the active crater, head up to the lookout over Botos Lake, an ancient, inactive crater, which is now filled with rainwater. The giant-leafed plants dotted along the way are known as *sombrillas de pobre* (poor man's umbrellas).

As you come back down the path from the crater, you will find the entrance to the **Sendero de la Escalonia** (Stepping Stone Trail) not far from the picnic tables. This path leads you through an enchanting tropical wonderland of mosses, bromeliads, ferns, and flowers. Your English-Spanish dictionary will help you decipher the poetry carved on signs along the trail. There is also a visitors' center with a gift shop, an interesting insect exhibit, and a cafe in which you can replenish your energy levels before continuing.

Guided Horseback Tour

In the unlikely event that you arrive at Poás only to find that the park has been closed due to toxic emissions, alternative ways to spend the morning include a guided horseback ride or a hike through the countryside surrounding the park. You can rent horses from **Finca Las Lagunillas**, near the park entrance. The turnoff to the *finca* is about 2.5km (1½ miles) below the park entrance,

and from there, another 1km (½ mile) down a steep dirt road. Park at the sign that reads 'Lagunilla Lodge – 400 meters' and walk in. If you are tempted by either the guided horseback tour or the hike, the prices are fairly reasonable in both cases.

On the way back down the road to Alajuela, you might pause at a roadside stand to buy strawberry preserves or cookies, both made by local women. Continue on to Chubascos restaurant for lunch. Sitting indoors or out, you might order *casado* (the dish of the day) and *fresas en leche* (a local drink similar to strawberry milkshake).

After the Chubascos stop it is time to head for the **Butterfly Farm** (daily 9am–3pm; tel/fax: 438-0115; email: butterflies@butterflyfarm.co.cr; admission charge). Given that this is the second-largest such farm in the world – some 500 different species of butterfly are raised for export here – the admission charge seems reasonable. To get there from Alajuela you should drive south toward the airport. At the traffic lights by Pereferico's turn right, and about 275 meters (300 yards) later take the first left. From here it is just over 10km (6 miles) away, passing through the small settlements of Villa Bonita, El Roble, and Ciruelas. At the T-junction in the center of Guácima, turn right and then left. From here, follow the signposts to the Butterfly Farm. In the course of a fascinating two-hour tour you will learn all about the butterfly's life cycle. You will, of course, also get the rare opportunity to see and photograph hundreds of different species of live butterflies. If you get hungry while you are here, the Blue Crowned Motmot restaurant in the grounds of the Butterfly Farm is highly recommended.

Above: one of 500 species of butterfly at the world's second-largest butterfly farm

The
Caribbean Coast

The country's Caribbean coast is populated primarily by Creole English-speaking blacks, ethnic Chinese, and indigenous people, many of whom live on reserves. Spanish is spoken, but it is a second language for many. The main centres of tourism in this region are the Tortuguero and Cahuita national parks, the village of Puerto Viejo, and the stunning, palm-lined beaches of the Talamanca coast between Cahuita and the border with Panamá. Puerto Limón is a port town with a shady reputation that is worth seeing only in Carnival Week (mid-Oct), when the parade involves hundreds of locals in bright costumes dancing and making music on the streets.

It is quite easy to get around the Talamanca coast by car. The Atlantic Coast Highway from San José, through the delightful scenery of the Parque Nacional Braulio Carrillo – incorporating mountains, waterfalls, canyons, and virgin forest – is in reasonable condition, and the route is straightforward. If you don't want to drive or hire a driver or car, there are comfortable express buses from San José to Puerto Limón, from where you can catch local buses to Cahuita and Puerto Viejo.

Wildlife Viewing

Tortuguero's village and park are not accessible by land, but a guided boat ride up the remote jungle canals to the park (leaving from Moín) is truly memorable. The best way to view the canals' wildlife is to arrange a trip with expert naturalist guides, such as Fran and Modesto Watson *(see page 36 for details)*, but alternative options for adventurous travelers include hitching a ride on a cargo boat, or renting a dugout canoe or even a speedboat.

The park, which covers some 19,000 hectares (47,000 acres), is a haven for turtles. The name Tortuguero derives from the Spanish word *tortuga* (turtle) and if you are here during the turtle breeding season (July–Sept) you may see female turtles nesting in the sand or baby turtles emerging from their nests.

On returning to Moín, you c an continue your travels on the Caribbean coast or return to San José. It's a good idea to head south to Puerto Viejo, away from the crowded capital to beaches that are unsurpassed: the water is turquoise, warm, and clear, and the beaches are sandy, white, and palm-fringed. Puerto Viejo is renowned in surfing circles for the Salsa Brava wave that breaks over the reef in June and July and from December through April.

Right: homes in Puerto Limón

6. PARQUE NACIONAL TORTUGUERO *(see map, p38)*

A two-day guided tour of Tortuguero's jungle canals and the village where sea turtles nest on the beaches.

Contact the Watsons (tel/fax: 226-0986; e-mail: fvwatson@sol.racsa.co.cr; www.members.tripod.com/FrancescaTours) and make an advance reservation for the Francesca, *a canopied fiberglass boat. This tour includes transfers, boat tours, lodging and five meals. A three-day, two-night tour is also available. For this trip to the hot and humid coastal region, bring an overnight bag packed with lightweight clothing, a pair of shoes suitable for walking on wet, muddy trails, mosquito repellent, sunscreen, and a protective hat.*

Situated in the country's most northeastern corner, **Parque Nacional Tortuguero** is the main nesting area in the western Caribbean for green sea turtles, which are attracted to its vast, open, windswept beaches. The park, which is not accessible by land, is reached by an extraordinary system of waterways that provide an excellent opportunity for observing the region's abundant flora and fauna. Recommended stopover options include Mawamba Lodge (www.grupomawamba.com), Pachira Lodge (www.pachiralodge.com) and Laguna Lodge (www.lagunalodgetortuguero.com).

Modesto and Fran Watson are highly experienced guides. They know the canals intimately, and, with their trained and knowledgeable eyes, the shy inhabitants of the jungle and canals become visible: kingfishers, caimans, and assorted snakes emerge from the water lilies; freshwater turtles surface on logs in the canals; howler monkeys, spider monkeys, toucans, and sloths appear in the trees overhead. This is a personal tour, conducted by affable people who know and love the jungle. Fran and Modesto will pick you up in San José at 6.30am and drive you to the wharf in Moín, on the Caribbean Coast, or you can meet them at the Moín dock at 9.30am. (Secure overnight parking is available at Moín for a small fee.) Leave behind any luggage that you don't need.

Beating Deforestation

The route from San José to Moín takes you through the majestic **Parque Nacional Braulio Carrillo**, which encompasses vast, misty mountains, dense primary forests, rivers, numerous waterfalls, two extinct volcanoes, and two small lakes. The park was founded in 1978 at the behest of environmentalists who feared that the construction of the highway from San José to the Caribbean coast would provide loggers with access to virgin forest, and lead to rapid deforestation of the area. You will stop for breakfast at Rio Danta, a pleasant open-air restaurant in a jungle setting. From there, it is about one hour through Atlantic-slope banana plantations to Moín.

Above: on the canal to Tortuguero
Above Right: a white egret looks for food. **Right:** a captive toucan makes itself heard

The river trip from Moín to Tortuguero on the *Francesca* is a leisurely three-hour ride. Keep an eye out for freshwater turtles and crocodiles basking in the canals, and for sloths, monkeys, toucans, macaws, parrots, and large blue morpho butterflies in the trees. Modesto's sharp eyes are a local legend – he will ease the boat into the river bank to get a better look at the monkeys he has spotted, or cut the engine in a particularly beautiful spot to allow you to appreciate the silence, and to see the turtles' heads poking out of the water and view the egrets in the trees.

You will arrive at Tortuguero's 35-km (22-mile) stretch of beach in time for a hearty late lunch at your lodge. Then visit the **Conservation Visitors Center** outside the village of Tortuguero. The center, which is run by the Caribbean Conservation Corporation (www.cccturtle.org) is the ideal place to learn about local wildlife, and to get laminated color plates of the birds of Costa Rica.

A Timeless Village

After visiting the center, take a walk through the village of Tortuguero (pop: 500). Narrow paths wind through exuberant greenery, palm trees rustle overhead, and wooden houses sit on stilts. Despite the conspicuous presence of modern restaurants, stores, and *cabinas* catering to tourists, to all intents and purposes traditional village life continues in a timeless way. After dinner at the lodge at 7pm, you will probably want to devote the evening to relaxation.

If it is the right time of year, however, turtles will be nesting on the beach, in which case you could join a guided walk to see these fascinating, gigantic creatures come out of the ocean to dig their nests in the sand. The enormous tractor-tread trails that they leave in the sand as they laboriously make their way up the beaches are easily visible, even at night under a stormy sky. Green sea turtles nest from July through mid-October, leatherbacks from March through June. Each female lays 100 or more golf-ball-size eggs

in a nest that she has dug out with her flippers. In undisturbed nests, the baby turtles hatch within a couple of months. Using a temporary egg tooth, they tear open their shells and soon the entire clutch is ready to rise to the surface. A critical mass of about 100 baby turtles all pulling together is needed to excavate the sand covering them. Usually just before dawn, they emerge onto the beach and scramble for the water. But the young reptiles are vulnerable to a number of dangerous enemies, including crabs, birds, sharks, and other predatory fish, as a result of which it is estimated that fewer than three percent of the baby turtles survive.

Those that do make it swim offshore to floating rafts of Sargassum weed, where they find shelter and food for their first and most difficult days at sea. For several decades green sea turtles live nomadic lives, migrating over vast distances in the open ocean. At about 50 years of age, they reach sexual maturity and reconvene on the beaches where they were hatched, to carry out the next stage in their reproductive cycle.

It is a good idea to have an early night because tomorrow's wildlife-spotting trip starts early. In the course of the trip you are likely to see toucans, macaws, coatis, anteaters, otters, and other animals. Return to the lodge for breakfast at 8am, and enjoy a couple of free hours, perhaps relaxing in a hammock at the lodge, or on the beach.

Great Turtle Mother

Alternatively, you could take a hike to **Cerro de Tortuguero** (Tortuguero Peak), a dormant volcano not far from the mouth of the river, which is believed to be a sacred Mayan site that honored the Great Turtle Mother, who called female turtles to the beach to make their nests. Some locals apparently believe that an unexcavated tunnel beginning at the base of the hill leads to a chamber where the Great Turtle Mother is protected by crocodiles. Although the hike up the hill is moderately strenuous, steep, and muddy, it is a worthwhile jaunt: from the top of the hill (the only high place in the area), you can see the canals winding through the jungle.

Reconvene at 10.30am for your return trip on the *Francesca*. Lunch is taken at a thatched-roof *rancho* along the river. The boat arrives at Moín in the early afternoon, and you will reach the Central Valley at around 6pm.

7. PUERTO VIEJO *(see map, p38)*

Staying at the Villas del Caribe hotel, swim and sunbathe at Punta Uva beach, join a horseback expedition, or take a guided hike into the jungle.

Pack bathing suit, sandals, tennis shoes, shorts, lightweight shirts, sunscreen, a sun hat, and a pair of long pants if you intend to ride horses. Cabina accommodation, covering the entire range from basic to luxurious, can be found opposite gorgeous stretches of white, sandy beach, edged by palm and almond trees. Villas del Caribe (tel: 233-2200; fax: 221-2801; www.villascaribe.net) is particularly delightful. A moderately priced condo-style hotel, it offers two-bedroom units with fully equipped kitchens. This location is suitable for both romantic getaways and for family vacations with children. Make reservations as far ahead as possible, especially in the Christmas and Easter holidays, and over weekends in the high season.

Until the 1970s this, the Talamanca region of the coast, was populated mainly by indigenous people in the mountains, and the descendants of English-speaking immigrants from the Caribbean along the coast. It was the latter who planted the coconut trees that line the beaches, and who developed the local culinary traditions. Hemmed in by the sea on one side and mountains on the other, they did not even have roads to the rest of the country.

Surfing and Partying

Since the opening of the highway from San José, lots of new *cabinas* and hotels have sprung up, and more and more foreign visitors come to enjoy the unspoilt beaches, wonderful surfing opportuni-

Above: the beaches are idyllic
Right: local transportation

ties, and laid-back party atmosphere. Just before the turnoff for Puerto Viejo is **Hone Creek**. Hone is the name of a short palm with large roots. The palm bears a fruit, also called a hone, from which the locals made cooking oil. Here there is usually a checkpoint, set up in an effort to stem the flow of contraband goods from Panamá. At Hone Creek, take the road to the left.

Snorkeling and Barbecues

Puerto Viejo (Old Harbor) is a small, Caribbean town 9 km (12 miles) south of Cahuita. Many visitors to the town are surfers wanting to experience the Salsa Brava wave that breaks over the reef between December and April and again in June and July. In the other months of the year the sea is quiet, and good for snorkeling. To the south are some of the country's finest beaches.

As you enter Puerto Viejo you will see a rusty barge moored off the black sand beach. Continue south through the town for about 4km (2½ miles) until you reach Villas del Caribe, whose entrance is announced by a large sign on the left. The rivers along the way are bridged by wooden planks without rails – take particular care when driving over these, especially when they are wet. Within easy walking distance of Villas del Caribe, a few kilometers to the south, is **Punta Uva**, a quintessential Caribbean beach where crystalline, tranquil water laps quietly on palm-lined beaches of white sand. Punta Uva is par-

ticularly good for swimming. Villas del Caribe rents out horses, snorkeling equipment, surf- and boogie boards, canvas beach chairs and hibachis (braziers) for barbecues.

If you want to take advantage of the self-catering facilities you should stock up on groceries. (Even if you don't want to cook main meals, you

Above: the condo-style Villas del Caribe
Left: at some beaches the sand is black

might want to enjoy breakfast on your balcony overlooking the beach.) Given the limited selection of groceries, especially vegetables, available in the village, it's a good idea to purchase provisions from a supermarket such as Mas por Menos before you leave the Central Valley. Don't forget to bring bottled water.

There are some fine eateries in and around Puerto Viejo, including pizzerias run by Italian immigrants. Other recommendations include Mi Modo, Shawanda, Garden Restaurant *(see restaurant listings, page 64)*, El Pescadito, and Carramba. If you would like to eat with a local family, ATEC *(see below)* can make recommendations. Alternatively ask around for Miss Dolly, Miss Sam or, for baked goods, Miss Daisy, who will be happy to prepare delicious meals for you so long as they have advance notice. When it comes to drinks, Restaurant Bambu is a popular place for cocktails while watching the exciting Salsa Brava waves. For entertainment later in the evening, Stanford's disco is open Thursday to Sunday nights, and Johnnie's Place is also good for dancing. Be warned that, after nightfall, for all the apparent tranquillity, it is inadvisable to walk alone on either the beach or on the road.

Ecotourism

In addition to swimming, surfing, boogie-boarding, cycling, and horseback-riding on the beach, there are some fabulous guided tours organized through the Talamancan Ecotourism and Conservation Association (ATEC) – a grass-roots community organization. ATEC's trained English- and Spanish-speaking guides conduct a wide range of nature walks and hikes focusing on Talamanca's natural history and culture. If you want to arrange a tour with ATEC, its offices are located opposite Soda Tamara in downtown Puerto Viejo. While there, it's a good idea to buy a copy of *Coastal Talamanca: A Cultural and Ecological Guide*. (If the office is closed, check out the website at www.greencoast.com//atec.htm or e-mail fordetailsatecmail@racsa.co.cr).

Another option is to ask in town for local guides. Recommended are Harry Hawkins, who specializes in medicinal herbs and Afro-Caribbean culture, and Martín Hernandez, who leads wildlife walks and ocean-diving tours. Further afield, local operator Atlantico Tours (tel: 750-0004), run by Ed Oliver, conducts tours to Tortuguero, Cahuita National Park, and Panama, as well as rafting and surfing trips.

Visitors interested in horticulture might like to spend some time at the **Botanical Gardens** (tel: 750-0046, email: jardbot@sol.racsa.co.cr) located close to El Pizote Lodge. Guided tours of the gardens take in an extensive collection of tropical flora – visitors can sample fruits that are in season before exploring the rainforest trail.

Right: sun hat and binoculars are essential

8. MANZANILLO   *(see map, p38)*

A cycle ride from Puerto Viejo to the sleepy village of Manzanillo, where you can join an excursion in a motorized dugout canoe.

Bring a bottle of water, sunscreen, sun hat, bathing suit, and suitable shoes for hiking. Rent your bicycle the previous day to get an early start. Try Damari's in Puerto Viejo; David at the hardware store at the entrance to Punta Cocles; the Playa Chiquita Lodge (tel: 233-6613) about 6km (4 miles) south of Puerto Viejo; or Soda y Restaurante Naturales, on the same road as the lodge.

Manzanillo is a fishing village 14km (9 miles) from Puerto Viejo at the end of the coastal road. En route from Puerto Viejo, you pass through the **Refugio Nacional de Vida Silvestre Gandoca-Manzanillo** (Gandoca and Manzanillo Wildlife Reserve), which stretches from south of Puerto Viejo to the Panamá border. The reserve covers 5,000 hectares (12,500 acres) of land and 4,500 hectares (11,000 acres) of sea and incorporates a 5-sq-km (2-sq-mile) coral reef that is rich in tropical marine life. Most of the reserve is flat or has gently rolling hills covered with forest, grassland, and farms, but hiking is limited to the coast.

Local Flavor

Willie Barton (also known as Mr Willie), a respected community healer and fisherman, is the ideal person to take you out either on the ocean in his motorized dugout canoe, or for a medicinal-herb walk along the coastal trail. Mr Willie's house, recognizable by its veranda, is the last building at the south end of the village. When you ask him to take you out in his canoe, or for a walk, make arrangements with his wife, Miss Marva – who has established a reputation as an excellent cook – to have lunch ready for you when you get back. If walking, you might well want to stop along the way for a swim in the ocean, or for a cold drink at one of the *sodas* or *pulperias* (little grocery stores) along the way.

Central
Pacific Beaches

Costa Rica's hundreds of kilometers of Pacific coastline feature beaches and accommodations options of every description. In the northern **Guanacaste Province** there are innumerable sandy stretches and resorts. Here, at the surfers' paradise of **Playa Grande**, are friendly, personal places such as Las Tortugas Hotel. Overlooking **Playa Ocotal** you will find, perched on a hill, the secluded luxury resort of El Ocotal. Catering to visitors' special interests, the Nosara Retreat, an elegant mansion on **Playa Nosara**, features yoga classes and vegetarian meals. And of course there are large resort hotels, at **Playa Conchal**, **Playa Flamingo**, and **Playa Tambor**.

To the south of the region are quiet beaches that are perfect for surfers and swimmers. Of these, **Manuel Antonio** makes for a particularly good beach holiday. Its sands are outstandingly beautiful, and it is close to the jungle and the town of Quepos, with its nightlife, restaurants, and shops. Unlike many of the country's beach resorts, Manuel Antonio is accessible by car, bus, or plane. From the Central Valley, the journey takes over three hours by car, about four hours by bus, and 20 minutes by plane. If sunbathing on sparkling white-sand beaches, body surfing, ocean kayaking, horseback riding, and hiking in the jungle (with some live music and dancing at night) are on your agenda, Manuel Antonio is the perfect destination.

Scenic Routes

If you are driving, there are two routes to Manuel Antonio from the Central Valley, either via the new highway (which is generally in good condition but can be crowded) leading through Atenas and Orotina, or on the quieter old highway to the Pacific, through Ciudad Colón, the Quítirrisi Indian Reserve, and Santiago de Puriscal. Both routes are scenic, and both offer interesting stops along the way. Driving time for each is approximately 3½ hours. If you want to explore the Central Pacific zone more fully before arriving at Manuel Antonio, take the old highway into the countryside and stay in a renovated farmhouse on Masatal, a large wilderness preserve close to the old highway to the Pacific. At Masatal, you can explore the forest, accompanied by a guide if desired, and ride horses.

If you have time to visit Quepos en route to Manuel Antonio (7km/4 miles away), you will discover the flavor of an old-time fishing and banana town. Though the town has seen better days, there are decent hotels and restaurants, and transport to Manuel Antonio. In both towns, prior reservations are essential for all accommodations, whatever in the price, in the holiday season.

Left: a simple local fishing technique
Right: surf's up on southern Pacific beaches

9. THE OLD HIGHWAY
TO THE PACIFIC & MASATAL *(see map below)*

This beautiful route passes through unspoilt mountain terrain. You can spend the night in a pleasant farmhouse at the Masatal wilderness preserve and follow its trails to waterfalls and swimming holes.

Bring hiking shoes, a sun hat, sunblock, a swimsuit, and a change of clothing. Driving time is approximately 2½ hours so make an early start.

Take the highway west toward Santa Ana and Ciudad Colón. After Ciudad Colón, the road winds through the Quítirrisi Indian Reserve, where foodstuff such as honey, baskets, and other handmade goods can be purchased at roadside stands. Several kilometers up the road on the left, you will see a produce stand and some unpainted houses. If you want to sample *tamales* (dough filled with a traditional mix of pork, rice, olives, and carrots) or have a drink of warm *aqua dulce* (sweet water), this is a good place to stop.

The farming town of **Santiago de Puriscal**, with its beautiful church and large central park, is the last outpost of city life before Parrita on the Pacific Coast. After the church, ask for directions to **Parrita**. Beyond Puriscal the road is unpaved but is generally in good condition. The road wends its way through mountains and valleys, small farms and settlements. The absence of traffic makes driving here a real pleasure.

Above: Puesta del Sol

To Masatal

Some 15 minutes after Puriscal, in the village of **Santa Marta**, look for a huge bougainvillea tree on the left. Underneath it is a *soda* (a cafe), where you can stop for breakfast or a snack. Then continue to the village of Salitrales, near which is the turn-off to **Masatal**. When you book your rooms at Masatal (by calling Puesta del Sol Country Inn on 289-8775) you should be given explicit directions, and arrangements will be made for you to collect the key from the caretaker. The moderate rates include breakfast.

Masatal is a privately owned wilderness preserve that protects hundreds of hectares of tropical mountains, valleys, and rivers. The property, located near a small rural settlement, features a pleasant three-bedroom farmhouse with wide verandas and expanses of lawn. You can negotiate its well-maintained trails, which run through primary and secondary forest, either on your own or guided by Masatal's caretaker, Chepo. Monkeys, toucans, parrots, coatis, armadillos, pumas, and countless species of bird and butterfly frequent the area. Horses are also available for riding. The chef, Pierre Coutou, will prepare an elegant picnic lunch for you on request.

To get to Manuel Antonio for the next itinerary, continue to the village of Gloria, where the road begins its descent to sea level. Once at the coast, head south to Parrita, and onward to Quepos and Manuel Antonio.

10. PARQUE NACIONAL MANUEL ANTONIO *(see map p44)*

Hike in the national park, where wide, white sandy beaches meet the jungle. Try ocean kayaking and horseback riding in the jungle.

Book your hotel room and any necessary transportation early, especially during Easter and Christmas holidays. Bring mosquito repellent, walking shoes, plus swimsuit, sun hat, sunblock, towel, a good book, shorts, shirts, and sandals for the beach, and something more dressy for a night out.

If you are not coming from Masatal, Travelair (tel: 220-3054) runs 20-minute flights from San José to Quepos, from where a taxi can take you to your hotel in the town of Manuel Antonio. **Manuel Antonio National Park** (Tues–Sun 8am–4pm; admission charge), which consists of 680 hectares (1,680 acres) of primary forest, swamps, and tropical woodlands, is one of the country's smallest. The coastline is its true glory – three long strands of white sandy Pacific Ocean beach are fringed by jungle on one side. They are clean and wide and especially good for swimming. Above them monkeys, sloths, and many other animals and birds inhabit the tall cliffs' jungle vegetation. To protect the park's eco-systems, the rangers admit a maximum of 600 people on weekdays, 800 on weekends.

You can travel between beach, town, and hotel quite easily by taxi or bus, or you can rent a car. And there are lots of accommoda-

Right: the coati is akin to a Central American raccoon

tions options – the road into the park is lined with hotels and *cabinas*. The hotels on one side of the road are built into the hill above the beach and offer stunning ocean views. On the other side the hotels poke out of the trees and vegetation. Don't be surprised to receive a 5am wake-up call from the resident howler monkeys..

On the jungle side of the road the Hotel Casitas Eclipse (tel/fax: 777-0408) has beautiful, white, Mediterranean-style villas and three tiled swimming pools. A lower-price option is the Naturalist Beachfront Apart-hotel (tel/fax: 777-1475), one of the few places in Manuel Antonio to be built on the sand. Both places have kitchens, and friendly resident owners.

There is no shortage of things to do and see in Manuel Antonio. You might head down the road to Espadilla Beach and have an early breakfast at one of the open-air *sodas* along the beachfront just before the park entrance, which is a 15-minute walk away from the Eclipse. When the tide is out you can walk onto the park beaches, but it is not advisable to cross at high tide, when the water can be waist-high. At the park entrance, pay the (reasonable) admission charge and continue south to the first beach, **Espadilla del Sur**. Next is **Manuel Antonio Beach**, which provides a perfect place for a swim and has a path that leads up to Cathedral Point. Beyond Manuel Antonio Beach is **Puerto Escondido**, but this beach becomes almost completely submerged at high tide.

For a less strenuous morning, walk, drive, or catch a bus down to Espadilla Beach to rent a beach umbrella and stretch out on the sand. (You can park in the shade of the trees near Mar y Sombra, but make sure that you lock the car.) Be warned that Espadilla Beach sometimes has rip tides – strong ocean currents that can carry swimmers out beyond the breakers. If you want to swim, take the safe option and walk north a little way along the beach.

Iguana Tours (tel: 777-1267; fax: 777-2052) arranges river-rafting trips, coastal cruises, deep-sea fishing trips, and other adventures. After dark, try the Bahia Azul or the Arco Iris in Quepos for more local color. Quepos's casinos are at the Hotel Kamuk, the Divisamar, and the Parador.

The South

The southern region was one of the last areas of the country to be settled, and in many ways it remains Costa Rica's final frontier. For the first 300 years of the country's recorded history, the Talamanca Mountains seemed to present an impenetrable barrier to settlement of the southern zone, but in 1860 a mountain pass was discovered and the southern region became accessible. The opening of the road led to the colonization of the Valle de El General and the building of the Interamerican Highway, which connects San José and the Central Valley with the Southern Pacific area. The south is home to proportionally more national parks and forest reserves than anywhere else in the country. It is also one of the least visited regions.

On the way south from San José, the road ascends toward the spectacular **Cerro de la Muerte** (Mountain of Death). This, the highest mountain pass on the highway, was named after early travelers who died from either exposure to the elements or hunger while crossing the mountain. The route descends into the cool cloud forests of San Gerardo de Dota, where there is a good chance of spotting that most legendary of birds, the resplendent quetzal.

Farther south is **Cerro Chirripó** (which, at 3,820 meters/12,530ft, is the country's highest mountain), the **Golfo Dulce** (with its free-port city of **Golfito**), and the magnificent **Península de Osa**. This wild, imposing peninsula features pretty, sandy beaches, rocky headlands, and rivers and streams that cascade over cliffs. But its biggest attraction is the **Parque Nacional Corcovado**, which is home to the country's most majestic forests.

A Base for Exploration

A good way to explore the Península de Osa is from a base on the northeastern edge, at **Bahía Drake** (Drake Bay). This is said to be the place where Sir Francis Drake, the first English explorer to circumnavigate the world, landed in 1579. There are several good lodges in the area, whose staff will be happy to help with your travel arrangements: such assistance can be very useful because getting around here can present complex logistical problems.

But don't let that deter you from making the most of this region, which presents the opportunity to experience some thrilling adventures. Staying at La Paloma Lodge for instance, you can take guided hikes for wildlife-spotting in the wilds of Corcovado's virgin rainforest; join a snorkeling expedition to the important pre-Columbian archaeological site of Isla del Caño; paddle upriver in a kayak; or explore the jungle on horseback, accompanied by an experienced local guide.

Above Left and **Left:** at Manuel Antonio
Right: proceeding at a slow pace

11. SAN GERARDO DE DOTA *(see pull-out map)*

A two-day trip to the cloud forest of San Gerardo de Dota, where you should see the hemisphere's most magnificent bird, the elusive quetzal.

Book ahead with Savegre River Mountain Inn (tel: 771-1732). Bring hiking shoes, and warm clothing, because it gets cold at night. To get there, you can rent a car, hire a driver, or take the bus heading to San Isidro. The turnoff to San Gerardo de Dota is located at KM80 on the Interamerican Highway, and it's a further 8km (5 miles) along a bumpy dirt road to the inn. The bus stops a scenic two- to three-hour walk away from the albergue turnoff, though someone from the Albergue will pick you up for a fee.

From the Central Valley, the route passes over the spectacular Cerro de la Muerte (Mountain of Death), which rises to 3,350 meters (11,000ft). If you need a refreshment break, stop at the intersection store and *soda* at Empalme. Not far from here is the former home of the late president, José Figueres. Rain, cold, and fog can make the first part of the trip somewhat unpleasant, but after a while the road emerges above the clouds. Thereafter, the sunshine is usually brilliant, the air cool and crisp, and the surrounding fields of flowers and hillside farms quite picturesque. The clouds swirling through the valleys, and the patches of purple foxgloves, azaleas, and cala lilies are in themselves reason enough to make this trip.

Shy but Famous

The quetzal (which is often described as 'resplendent') is Central America's most famous bird. The ancient Mayans called it the 'bird of life.' Under the impression that it would not live in captivity, they thought it symbolized freedom. And they prized its long, iridescent green tail feathers more highly than gold. The ornithologist Alexander Skutch writes of the quetzal: 'The pigeon-sized male owes his elegance to the

Above: the Mountain of Death
Right: the resplendent quetzal

intensity and brilliant contrasts of his colors, the sheen and glitter of his plumage, the beauty of his adornments, and the noble dignity of his posture.'

In addition to its radiant green plumage, the bird has a luminous crimson breast, yet it is a difficult bird to spot. It lives in the cloud forests and eats *aguacatillo* – a small fruit related to the avocado. Many travelers flock to the cloud forests of Monteverde in the Central Pacific zone to spot quetzals, but they often leave disappointed. San Gerardo de Dota presents a far better chance of seeing the bird because *aguacatillos* grow here. Quetzals are most abundant and easiest to spot during their nesting season (March–May).

The Albergue de Montaña Río Savegre (Savegre River Mountain Inn), which is run by the hospitable Chacón family, features simple, clean *cabinas*, all of which have private baths. Apples, plums, and peaches grow on the owner's farm and the banks of the creeks are thick with watercress. The *albergue* does good food – the room rate includes three meals a day. Guided hikes on offer include the trail to Cerro de la Muerte, with its fabulous views of the valleys, and there are less strenuous hikes through the Chacón family's estate or down San Gerardo's country roads. Anglers should appreciate the opportunity to catch trout in the Río Savegre.

12. BAHIA DRAKE *(see map, p50)*

Visit the remote, majestic Península Osa for a trip down the Sierpe River to Bahía Drake on the Pacific.

Bring boots, insect repellent, and a flashlight. See main text for information on getting there and places to stay.

Located in an area of spectacular natural beauty, **Bahía Drake** (Drake Bay) is situated on the northeastern coast of the **Península Osa**. Its inaccessibility is such that you can get there only by boat or plane. The rocky coastline is dotted with sandy coves and tall palms, the blue waters of the Pacific Ocean fluctuating between a deep indigo color and a luminous aquamarine, as the sunlight and clouds come and go. The green hills of the jungle rise up sharply behind the beach, and provide homes to squirrel monkeys, capuchin monkeys, scarlet macaws, parrots, and scores of other exotic bird species.

Getting to Drake Bay

The best way to get to Drake Bay is to make reservations at one of the area's lodges and allow the lodge's staff to handle the rather complicated travel arrangements required to get there. The first leg of the journey involves a flight to the airstrip at Palmar, in the Osa Peninsula. Flights can be arranged from San José and Quepos. From Palmar, you will travel overland through banana and palm plantations to the town of Sierpe on the calm,

Right: a bromeliad rises from the undergrowth in the jungle

muddy Sierpe River, and from there, by boat downriver to the Pacific. Here you will find mangroves growing along the river's edge, and lavender-colored water hyacinth thriving in the water. Watch out for the crocodiles that lurk beneath the surface. Once you arrive at the Pacific, your boatman will negotiate the incoming surf before proceeding through the waters of the ocean en route to Drake Bay.

Of the numerous places to stay at Drake Bay, La Paloma Lodge (tel: 239-2801), a friendly, well-run operation built into the hillside above the bay, is a good option. You have to climb a rather steep hill to get to there, or you can get a ride on the lodge's tractor. The rustic bungalows, which are rather like treehouses, extend out over the ocean. They can accommodate up to five people and are simple, pleasant, and clean. Double rooms, equipped with bathrooms and decks with views, are a less expensive option.

After lunch at the lodge, head down the hill to Playa Cocolito, the local beach, or swim in the pool and relax on the deck overlooking the ocean. If you would like to go on a guided sunset horseback ride on the day of your arrival, ask the proprietors of the lodge to arrange it for you when you make your reservations.

At about 6pm guests congregate in the open dining room for drinks and a discussion about their day's adventures. Dinner starts at 7pm, and conversations frequently linger long into the evenin, under a brilliant starry sky, accompanied by the sound of the surf on the beach below. At breakfast, you are likely to spot parrots, scarlet macaws, and capuchin monkeys in the giant balsa tree not far from the dining area.

Wildlife-Spotting

After breakfast, you can set out on a hiking and wildlife-spotting expedition into the **Parque Nacional Corcovado** *(see Itinerary 13, below)*, or you

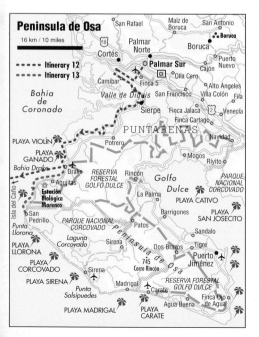

could go snorkelling and exploring in the **Reserva Biológica Isla de Caño** (Caño Island Biological Reserve), an important archaeological site 19km (12 miles) west of the lodge, a pleasant one-hour boat ride away. Caño was a pre-Columbian burial ground and its attractions include two mysterious stone spheres, which remain half-buried in the undergrowth at the highest point of the island. Thousands of spheres like these have been found in many locations in the south of Costa Rica and a few also in northern Panamá. They pose one of the country's great riddles. It is speculated that they were made in villages on the Osa Peninsula near Palmar Norte, brought

Palmar Norte, brought to Caño in canoes, then rolled to the top of the cemetery. Smaller stone spheres, which are the size of oranges, were possibly toys but the huge spheres, over 2 meters (6 ft) in diameter, may have indicated the political or social standing of the deceased.

Wildlife is scarce on the island but there are several coral reefs, which offer opportunities for good snorkeling. Brilliantly-colored tropical fish are easily seen by skin divers within 15 meters (50ft) of the shore. Between December and April 40-ton humpback whales come from their feeding grounds in Alaska, and you may spot them on your boat ride over to the island. Paloma Lodge guests are invited to fish from the boat for the evening's dinner: yellowtail tuna, dorado, and wahoo are common varieties. Fishing enthusiasts can also arrange for sport fishing charters. The bill-fishing season is late January through March. Scuba diving excursions can also be arranged.

13. PARQUE NACIONAL CORCOVADO   *(see map, p50)*

Take a boat trip along the Osa Peninsula's beautiful, rocky coastline and join a guided tour of the vast Corcovado National Park's virgin rainforest. A picnic lunch is followed by a hike to San Pedrillo Waterfall.

Bring good boots, water, sunscreen, a sun hat, insect repellent, swimsuit, binoculars, a camera and, during the rainy season, a poncho.

Parque Nacional Corcovado, which covers around 42,000 hectares (100,000 acres) on the remote **Península Osa**, protects one of the earth's richest and most diverse tropical regions. This is the natural habitat of some 500 species of tree, 10,000 species of insect, hundreds of species of bird, plus frogs, lizards, turtles, and many of the world's most endangered and spectacular mammals, including ocelots, pumas, jaguars, and tapirs.

Prior to its establishment as a national park in 1975, the Corcovado area was inhabited by loggers, *oreros* (gold panners), and farmers given government grants to 'improve' the land. In pre-Columbian times, the Diquis Indians, who were known for their beautiful gold work, lived in this region. The Spanish made repeated incursions into the peninsula in search of gold; on failing to find the leg-

Above: a parrot in its natural habitat
Right: jaguar at Corcovado National Park

endary Veragua mines, they plundered the natives' gold.

The mines were never located, but the rumours persist. In the 1980s, when the country was suffering an economic depression, there were so many *oreros*, causing such serious environmental damage, that the civil guard was called in to remove them. There are still *oreros* in the park, but hunters are the rangers' biggest adversary. With the advent of eco-tourism, many ex-*oreros* and hunters have found new careers as rangers and guides.

This itinerary is based on a guided trip to Corcovado organized by La Paloma Lodge, which provides transportation, lunch, and an English-speaking guide. It is generally done every other day. Departing from the lodge at about 7am, events begin with a 30-minute boat ride in the open ocean, from Drake Bay south to the ranger station in San Pedrillo.

The hike into Corcovado from the station takes about three hours. It is not strenuous, and the pace is kept deliberately slow to optimize the opportunities for wildlife-spotting, but there are steep ascents and descents, and the trail can be rough. Hiking boots with good traction help to prevent slips and falls, though some hikers prefer thick, rubber, calf-length boots as a protection against snake bites – which are rare.

Virgin Rainforest

The coastal area around San Pedrillo was deforested before it became national parkland, and the early part of the hike is through dense, 25-year-old secondary forest. Hiking inland you enter virgin (primary) rainforest, comprised of gigantic old trees with huge buttress roots, covered in epiphytes and large vines. The forest floor is cool and shady. Look out for butterflies, leaf-cutter ants and their enormous nests, and fungi in many different colors. The hike heads south to the **Río Pargo**, then west to the beach. Once back at the station, the grassy area above the beach is a great spot for a picnic lunch.

The lovely sandy beach in front of the ranger station is a great place to swim, sunbathe, or nap under the trees. If you have the energy, you could set off on a short hiking expedition to **San Pedrillo Falls**. The trail to the falls is quite rough, but not difficult or strenuous. On the way back you might stop for a swim in the river. Continue walking in the river – in the right direction – and you will arrive back at the station. The boat will pick you up at around 2pm, returning you to the lodge in time for a pre-prandial drink or nap – or a kayak paddle up the **Río Agujitas**.

Top: watch out for low-flying red-eyed tree frogs when exploring the jungle
Above: the rainforest's dense vegetation conceals myriad wonders of nature

The North

The lush, verdant landscape to the north of San José rolls along the Cordillera Central (Central Mountain Range). The tropical climate here is cooler than elsewhere in the country, and the terrain is greener. This is agricultural country, with meadows and farms rather than jungles, and well-kept, relatively prosperous towns in the mountains.

Driving through the region, you are bound to notice a tidy tranquillity that contrasts with the more chaotic atmosphere of the coastal regions. **Grecia**, for example, has been a candidate for the title of cleanest town in the world. You will pass lots of neat houses, in front of which stand small kiosks that sell homegrown produce, such as homemade cheese, *natilla* (sour cream), cookies, and preserves. Gorgeous dahlias, roses, and peach trees grow in the yards. The town of **Sarchí** is known for its carpenters, hence the many furniture and souvenir shops. **Zarcero** has an extraordinary central park filled with cypress topiary sculpted by the town's gardener.

Ring of Fire

To the north the city of **Ciudad Quesada** (also known as San Carlos due to its proximity to the San Carlos Plains) prospers from the region's agricultural productivity, and surrounding the city you will find orchards, plantations, and ranches. Northwest of San Carlos, in the **Cordillera de Guanacaste** (Guanacaste Mountains), lie seven volcanoes (Orosi, Cerro Cacao, Rincón de la Vieja, Santa María, Miravalles, Tenorio, and Cerro Jilguero), some of which are active and smoking. Just south of these is the spectacular **Volcán Arenal**, one of the world's most active volcanoes, and the destination for Itinerary 14. When Arenal vents its anger, red-hot lava and huge boulders cascade down its slopes.

In the area around Arenal you can explore hot springs, waterfalls, caves, and the beautiful **Laguna de Arenal** (Lake Arenal), in which the image of the quintessentially cone-shaped volcano is reflected. The lake attracts fishermen hoping to catch *guapote* (a rather spectacular-looking fresh-water fish). Its western end has in recent years become an important destination for windsurfers who come from countries allover the world.

Located in the country's far north, close to the border town of Los Chiles, are the **Río Frío** (Cold River) and **Refugio Nacional de Vida Silvestre Caño Negro** (Black Cane Wildlife Refuge), which is one of the most biodiverse areas in the country. Itinerary 15 is a birding and wildlife-watching tour of this remote and inaccessible region.

Right: fishing in Laguna de Arenal

14. VOLCAN ARENAL *(see map below)*

Drive through the lush northern zone to see one of the world's most active volcanoes, and have a soak in Tabacón's therapeutic waters.

The Arenal area is relatively warm, but bring a sweater for the evenings and a swimsuit if you want to sample the hot springs.

Until 1968, **Volcán Arenal** was an unremarkable, heavily wooded, low hill near the village of La Fortuna, then one morning locals began to feel slight earth tremors. Over a period of a few weeks, the forest smoked and steamed, and women washing clothes in the creeks marveled at the increasingly warm water. Then, on July 29, Arenal exploded. The shock waves were recorded thousands of kilometers away and some 5 sq km (2 sq miles) of land were transformed from pastoral farmland to a torturous, otherwordly landscape.

Since then, Arenal has remained continuously active. It is the quintessential volcano: conical, rising sharply out of flatland vegetation, its image reflected in the waters of **Laguna de Arenal** (Lake Arenal). Nights are especially good for volcano viewing – the red-hot lava and boulders pouring from the cone stand out in dramatic relief against the dark sky. Even if Arenal happens to be shrouded in clouds, the roar and rumble of boulders tumbling down its slopes on an otherwise balmy and silent night is truly memorable.

Volcano Views

Set high on a ridge facing Arenal, the **Arenal Observatory Lodge** (tel: 257-9489) offers stunning views of the erupting volcano. Many of the rooms are designed in such a way that you can see the volcano from your bed. Prices range from expensive to very expensive, and include substantial breakfasts and dinners in the lodge's dining room. For less expensive but pleasant *cabinas* with volcano views, try Jungla y Senderos Los Lagos (tel/fax: 479-9126). It is easy to reach the cabins by car. Rent a vehicle and drive through Grecia, Sarchí, Naranjo, and Ciudad Quesada (San Carlos). If you don't stop, the trip takes three to four hours. A good alternative is to call Carlos Mora (tel: 232-9870 or 384-4576) and arrange for him to take you; note that he charges for his own accommodation at the lodge. Carlos is familiar with the back roads and secret places: the waterfalls, the *sodas* with the best food, the trees where the sloths live, and the places where monkeys can sometimes be seen.

Either way, from San Carlos take the route through **Bajos del Toro** (Lowlands of the Toro River) with a stop for lunch at the Asociacíon Laboral de Mujeres Bajos del Toro, a cooperative of local women. The cornbread *(pan de elote)* is particularly recommended.

Continue through the pleasant village of La Fortuna (also known as Fortuna de San Carlos)

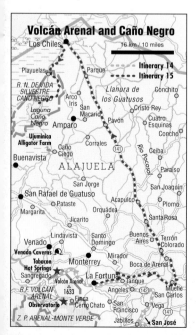

Volcán Arenal and Caño Negro

16 km / 10 miles

- - - Itinerary 14
- ● - Itinerary 15

Above Right: therapeutic waters at Tabacón
Right: an Arenal sunset

on the road to **Tabacón Hot Springs and Resort** (daily 7.30am–10pm for guests, 10am–10pm for non-guests; tel: 256-1500). This is the place for a relaxing soak in pools of every description and temperature, set in the midst of beautifully landscaped grounds. Massages and facial mud masks are available and there is a good restaurant and snack bar. You might decide to stay into the evening to watch the fireworks of the erupting volcano from the pools. The weather here is mercurial: clouds enshroud Arenal as quickly as they move away. Keep your fingers crossed for a clear night.

Leave Tabacón at about 7pm and head for your choice of accommodations for dinner. If you are staying at the Observatory Lodge head west for about 8km (5 miles) off the main highway, down a bumpy, gravel-and-dirt road.

There should be plenty of time in the morning for exploring the area. Although there is a small charge for day use of the observatory lodge's grounds, it's definitely worth the price if you are staying at the *cabinas*. The facilities include observation decks and rooms, and a museum complete with a seismograph that records the level of volcanic activity. You might also want to take advantage of the guided walks, which feature fantastic bird-watching opportunities, and paths that lead to outstanding natural attractions such as lava flows, a waterfall, and the Cerro Chata (dormant) volcano.

Dawn Balloon Flight

If you want to spend another day here, drive west along the lake shore to the village of Nuevo Arenal, for a visit to the **Jardín Botánico Arenal** (Arenal Botanical Gardens, closed Oct). Late in the afternoon is the optimum time to see the gardens, which were created by Michael Le May, an amateur horticulturist. Another exciting option is hot-air ballooning over the San Carlos Valley. Contact Costa Rica's ballooning specialist Serendipity Adventures (tel: 556-2592; fax 556-2593; email: costarica@serendipityadventures.com), which offers a trip into the sky just as the day is dawning and the countryside around Ciudad Quesada is waking.

15. REFUGIO NACIONAL CAÑO NEGRO *(see map, p54)*

A four-hour floating safari on the Río Frío to Caño Negro Wildlife Refuge through tropical rainforest, pastures, and marshlands. Observe abundant bird and animal life in one of Costa Rica's most remote areas.

Wear lightweight clothing, and bring mosquito repellent, a small bottle of drinking water, sun hat, and binoculars.

You can arrange an excursion to Caño Negro through either the Arenal Observatory Lodge *(see page 54)* or through Arenal Adventures (tel: 479-9133) – one of the major tour companies in La Fortuna. This itinerary is based on an Arenal Adventure safari, which includes an English-speaking guide, transportation, and lunch aboard the river boat in the price of a ticket.

Have an early breakfast, after which Arenal Adventures will pick you up from your lodge at about 7.30am. In the course of a drive of about 1½ hours, you will head east to La Fortuna, then north to Los Chiles, which is 3km (2 miles) from the border with Nicaragua. This is a rich agricultural area

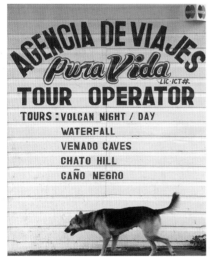

and on the way you will pass plantations and farms growing carob, cassava, plantain, oranges, sugar cane, papaya, beans, and rice – all mainstays of the traditional Costa Rican diet. You may see armed soldiers at the roadsides; these rural guards are on the look-out for migrants who have crossed the border at Los Chiles. According to some estimates there are more than 300,000 Nicaraguans living illegally in Costa Rica; their growing numbers pose considerable social and economic problems.

Along the Cold River

The covered-boat safari along the **Río Frío** (Cold River) commences at **Los Chiles**. You will probably see people fishing from the dock – the river is full of tarpon, snook, white drum, gar, and numerous other species. Some adult tarpon are said to weigh in at over 45kg (100lbs).

Refugio Nacional de Vida Silvestre Caño Negro (Caño Negro Wildlife Refuge) is one of Costa Rica's most inaccessible wildlife refuges. It covers approximately 10,000 hectares (25,000 acres), including **Laguna Caño Negro** , which expands to 800 hectares (nearly 2,000 acres) in the wet season, but almost disappears during the dry season. On your four-hour river trip you will pass through a diversity of habitats, including tropical rainforest, pasture, and marshlands. Along the way, you are likely to see a good range of wildlife – caimans, turtles, monkeys, iguanas, sloths, turtles, and lots of birds – including roseate spoonbills (sometimes mistaken for flamingoes) and jabiru, the largest bird of the region. In all, some 315 animal species have been identified here, including large cats.

Above: announcing the destinations of one of La Fortuna's tour companies
Right: a typically colorful Central American design

Leisure *Activities*

SHOPPING

Costa Rica is not a great destination for consumers. Imported goods and clothing are heavily taxed, limited in selection, and sometimes startlingly expensive. Shopping in downtown San José can be an unpleasant ordeal, compounded by crowds, traffic, and noise. For attractive gifts and souvenirs try the galleries, souvenir and gift shops in the Central Valley, and at artisans' stands in downtown San José.

In recent years **shopping malls**, often anchored by large supermarkets, have sprung up in the Central Valley. The stores, which cater to the affluent, sell imported clothing and shoes, domestic items, Spanish-language books, stationery items, and leather goods. The three-story **Mall San Pedro** (east of downtown San José, in San Pedro), billed as the country's biggest mall, has more than 200 stores, movie theaters, and a food court. Equally impressive is the **Multiplaza** mall just off the freeway on the route to Santa Ana, opposite the El Camino Real Hotel. **Real Mall Cariari**, on the General Cañas Highway, is the Central Valley's newest mall.

Costa Ricans tend not to bargain so there is little scope for haggling. You can try to get a discount but in most stores prices are fixed.

Environmentally conscious travelers should avoid buying coral, items made from tortoiseshell, furs, or items made from tropical hardwoods. The following list gives a few ideas of some typical Costan Rican things to buy.

Coffee

Costa Rican coffee is excellent and relatively inexpensive. Café Britt, recognized as one of the best types of coffee in the world, is available in supermarkets and gift shops in vacuum-packed bags. *Licor de Café Britt* is a coffee liqueur comparable – but superior – to Kahlua, which comes attractively packaged in a colorful gift box.

Cigars

Fine cigars made in Cuba, Costa Rica, Nicaragua, and Honduras are sold at Central Valley tobacco shops. To ensure freshness, buy from specialists rather than souvenir shops. Be wary of counterfeit Cuban cigars, and remember that it is illegal to take goods made in Cuba into the US.

Comestibles

Gift shops and supermarkets sell a variety of delicious salsa (try a Típica brand) and preserves. The most traditional local sauce, salsa lizano, is often eaten with *gallo pinto* (rooster, *see Eating Out, page 61*).

Fine Arts

Costa Rica is known for its fine arts, if not its folk crafts. The work of Costa Rican sculptors and painters is shown in many local galleries. See the What's Doing section of the *Tico Times* for details of current exhibitions. In San José, Galeria Namu (Avenida 7, Calles 5 & 7, tel: 256-3412) sells indigenous art and crafts.

Handmade Crafts

Woven bags and baskets dyed by Bribri Indians are sold at the Bookshop in San José's Barrio Amón, and at other stores downtown. Carved balsa-wood masks and gourds made by Boruca Indians are widely sold in gift shops. Handmade earrings and

Left: roadside vendor
Right: ceramics make good souvenirs

jewelry are inexpensive at the artisans' market in San José. Handmade papers and books made from recycled plant materials and dyed with natural substances are available in many gift stores.

Leather Goods

Leather bags, wallets, and briefcases are good buys in Costa Rica. There are fine leather stores in downtown San José and also in the newer shopping malls. Costa Rican shoes are generally inexpensive and well-made. Shoe stores abound in downtown San José and most feature a relatively wide selection of styles. Footwear imported from Columbia tends to be more refined, better-designed, and more expensive than its Costa Rican equivalents. Imported shoes are mostly found in the malls.

Wooden Items

Bowls, plates, cutting boards, boxes and the like are widely available from gift shops throughout the country. The mountain village of Sarchí is known for its woodwork, and the variety of wooden goods available in its many stores is impressive: here you will find everything from small wooden trinkets to hardwood rocking chairs, all packaged and ready to ship home. The prices in Sarchí are generally no lower than anywhere else, but the selection is large and the drive through the mountains to get there is lovely. Finer, better-crafted wooden pieces are made by Barry Biesanz of Biesanz Woodworks (tel: 228-1811; fax 228-6184; for directions and a map, see www.biesanz.com). The craftsman welcomes visitors to his light-filled studio in Bello Horizonte, near Escazú, but call first.

Above: fresh from the kiln
Right: carving a wooden figure

WHERE TO SHOP

San José
Atmosfera
Calle 5, Aveida 1–3
A well-displayed selection of folk art and fine crafts.

National Association of Independent Artisans
Calle 5, Avenida 4
Plaza de la Democracia
(just outside the National Museum)
Outside sales booths featuring interesting work by independent artisans.

Hotel Don Carlos Gift Shop
Calle 9, Aveida 9
Tel: 221-6707
Large souvenir shop.

Escazú
El Sabor tico
San Rafael de Escazú
(behind Plaza Colonial)
A fine selection of arts and crafts from all over Central America, displayed in an impressive setting.

Moravia
Souvenir shops and arts-and-crafts galleries line two blocks in the town center not far from the Red Cross (Cruz Roja). Items from the whole region of Central and South America, including textiles from Guatemala, woolen goods from the Andes, cigars from Nicaragua, and a wide assortment of other authentic items.

EATING OUT

Costa Ricans traditionally start the day with a steaming glass of *café con leche* (coffee with milk) and a hearty plate of *gallo pinto con huevo*. This traditional dish comprises black beans and fried rice seasoned with onions, sweet red peppers, and fresh *cilantro* (coriander leaf), with a fried egg on the side. *Gallo pinto* (literally: painted rooster) or *pinto*, is a revered national institution that seems somehow to taste best when eaten in small *sodas*.

It is customary for many Costa Ricans to go home for lunch, which is the major meal of the day. For working people who eat out, lunch usually consists of rice, black beans, cooked vegetables, a salad made with fresh cabbage, and a choice of chicken, meat, or eggs, all served together on one plate. This distinctive, tasty dish is known as *El Casado* – 'the married man's plate'.

The wonderful quality of the local fruit constitutes one of the great pleasures of eating in Costa Rica. *Ticos* tend to be very fond of fruit, and wherever you go you will see street vendors selling whatever happens to be in season at the time: papayas, pineapples, mangoes, avocados, *zapotes* (a sweet, soft local fruit), and *pejibayes* (also sometimes known as peach palms or peach nuts), to name just a few.

The majority of restaurants and cafes offer a variety of delicious drinks made from fresh fruit. These are called *naturales* or *frescos*. Among the tastiest are *maracuyá*, *cas*, and *guanabana*. Try a *mora en leche* (blackberries blended with milk, with a small quantity of ice and sugar added) or a creamy *papaya en leche* (papaya blended with milk). You might also want to sample the fresh ice creams at Pop's ice-cream stores.

In addition to establishments that serve traditional Costa Rican meals, the Central Valley has numerous excellent international restaurants. Many restaurants throughout the country are closed on Mondays, so always call ahead to check. All restaurants charge 13 percent sales tax and 10 percent service charge on top of the advertised price.

In the following recommendations, the prices indicated are the average cost of a meal for two:
$$$ = $50 plus, including wine
$$ = $25–$50, including wine
$ = $20, excluding wine

Central Valley
San José
Bijahua
La Granja, San Pedro
(near Mas por Menos)
Tel: 225-0613
Nouvelle Costa Rican cuisine, with many delightful surprises. In an elegant, subdued ambience, food is presented as art and entertainment. Impeccable service. $$$

Above: breakfast with a view

Cafe Mundo
Barrio Amon
Calle 15 , Avenida 9–11
Tel: 222-6190
A new restaurant that has a great atmosphere and a selection of international dishes, pizza and pasta. $$

El Chicote
North Sabana, Avenida Las Américas
Tel: 232-0936
Wonderful steaks, seafood and international dishes. $$

Fuji
Corobicí Hotel
(northeast corner of La Sabana)
Tel: 239-0033, ext: 191
This Japanese restaurant specializes in sushi, complete with eastern decor. You can try one of the Tatami-covered private dining rooms. $$$

El Exotico Oriente
Sabana West (not far from Canal 7)
Tel: 228-5980
Indonesian and Thai classics such as *satay* and *gado gado* (steamed vegetable salad with peanut sauce) served in what was once the living room of a family home. Friendly service. $$

Grano de Oro
Paseo Colón, Calle 30, Avenida 2–4
Tel: 255-3322
Dine on international cuisine in the attractive covered garden of one of San José's best, small hotels. Provides good food at breakfast, lunch, and dinner as well as friendly service. $$

La Cocina de Lena
Centro Comercial El Pueblo
Tel: 223-3704
La Cocina de Leña ('The Wood Stove') is situated in the popular entertainment and dining complex of El Pueblo and is one of the best-known restaurants for typical Costa Rican fare, including black bean soup, *gallo pinto, tamales,* and beef casado. The rustic atmosphere is complemented by frequent folk shows and music in high season. $$

La Princesa Marina
West Sabana
Tel: 232-0481
Excellent seafood at reasonable prices. Also branches in Moravia, Curridibat and Alajuela. $$

Lubnan
Paseo Colón (in front of Mercedes Benz)
Tel: 257-6071
Lebanese cuisine and classic Middle Eastern dishes. The sparse decor has an exotic, Levantine flavor. $$

Machu Picchu
Paseo Colón
Calle 32, Avenida 1–3
Tel: 222-7384
Fax: 225-2243
email: 201017@asstcard.co.cr
Good food at a Peruvian restaurant that has a casual, boisterous, ambience. On a night out, try a Pisco Sour and book a driver to get you home. $$

Cafe Ruiseñor at the Teatro Nacional
Downtown, in the National Theater
Tel: 225-2562
An elegant yet casual place to come for lunch, dessert or just a snack, complete with great espresso and cappuccino. White tablecloths, marble tables. An oasis of quiet in downtown San José. $

La Mazorca
San Pedro
(not far from Banco Anglo building)
Tel: 224-8069
San José's first vegetarian restaurant, which is popular with university students, serves fresh baked food in a casual ambience. $

Above: popular *comida tipica* fare

Little Seoul
Rohrmoser
Tel: 232-5551
Japanese and Korean joint specializing in sushi, Korean barbecues, and teppanyaki. $$

Los Antonojitos
Tel: 232-2411
A chain of Mexican-Tico restaurants found in several popular locations in San José and Escazu. Open daily, with mariachi bands on Friday and Saturday. $$

Soda Tapia
La Sabana Park (near the Gimnasio)
Tel: 222-6734
Gallo pinto, first-rate sandwiches, and delicious fruit drinks. Indoor tables and attractive patio. $

Spoon Cafe
Located in shopping malls and throughout downtown San José and Alajuela, these popular coffee-shops are known for their great selection of pastries, light lunches, coffees, and milk shakes. $

Tin Jo
C11, Avenida 6–8
Tel: 221-7605
The best downtown Asian restaurant does a selection of Thai, Chinese, Japanese, and Indian dishes. Elegant and cozy atmosphere in a former private residence. $$

Heredia
Hotel Chalet Tirol
Tel: 267-6226
www.arweb.com/tirol
email:tirolcr@sol.racsa.co.cr
Lovely French restaurant in rural setting. Beautiful walks near the hotel. Call ahead for directions. $$

Escazú/Santa Ana and San Antonio de Belén
Capriccio
San Rafael de Escazú
(300 meters/yds south of Perifericos)
Tel: 228-9332
Italian fare, including exceptional pastas and pizzas. Vegetarians might appreciate the offerings of an extensive antipasto buffet. $$

Chango
Escazú
Tel: 228-1173
International cuisine, steaks, and seafood. Sit indoors or outside on the covered veranda in this elegant yet friendly place. $$

Delmonico
Escazú
Tel: 228-9515
Excellent cuisine and sushi bar. $$$

Sale e Pepe
Escazú
Tel: 289-5750
Tasty Italian dishes. $$

La Cascada
Escazu
Tel: 228-0906
Seafood and grilled steaks. One of the best steakhouses in town. $$

Le Monastere
Escazu
Tel: 289-4404
This former chapel (hence the name) specializes in classic French cuisine plus interesting local dishes, and there are wonderful views of the volcanoes. Reservations recommended. $$$

Los Adobes
San Antonio de Belén
Tel: 239-0957
Costa Rican home-cooked food served up in a 100-year-old adobe building and its pleasant, covered patio. Live music on weekends. Casual atmosphere. $$

Right: Garden Restaurant, Puerto Viejo

Rancho Macho
Santa Ana
Situated in the hills above Santa Ana, you can dine on a porch overlooking the city's lights. Specialties are barbecued chicken and beef. Laid-back atmosphere. Musicians on some nights. $

Rosti Pollo
San Rafael de Escazú
Nicaraguan-style chicken and *Tres Leches* cake. Casual ambiance. Eat at a picnic table, or take your meal home. Fast service. $

Poás Volcano

Chubascos Restaurant
Fraijanes (1km/½ mile from the lake)
Tel: 482-2069
Local fare and tasty *refrescos* (fruit juices) served in a garden on the volcano slopes. $$

Central Pacific Beaches

La Fiesta del Maiz
La Garita de Alajuela
(en route from San José to the Central Pacific beaches)
Tel: 487-5757
Wide selection of dishes made from maize. Open weekends and high season only. $

Puerto Viejo

Garden Restaurant
Cabinas Jacaranda
Tel: 750-0069
Eclectic menu featuring beautifully prepared and presented Asian-Caribbean dishes. No credit cards and sometimes closed. $$

Manuel Antonio/Quepos

Barba Roja
Opposite Hotel Divisamar, Manuel Antonio
Tel: 777-6331
Authentic food in an attractive setting. $$

Café Milagro
Tel: 777-0794
Manuel Antonio
Tasty pastries, freshly roasted coffee and a nice place to relax. $

Karola's
Hotel Divisimar, Manuel Antonio
Tel: 777-1557
Mexican dishes and seafood served in a garden setting. Margaritas. $$

La Fonda Típica
In front of Tuany's, Manuel Antonio
Good Costa Rican food. $–$$

Rico Tico Bar & Grill
Si Como No Hotel, Manuel Antonio Park
Tel: 777-1250
Good American and local dishes. $$

El Gran Escape
Quepos
Friendly seafront restaurant specializing in Mexican fare. Hearty breakfasts. Closed Tuesday. $$

Jiuberths
Quepos (at the entrance to town)
Tel: 777-1292
Outstanding seafood. $$

Restaurante Isabel
Quepos (oceanfront)
Seafood and local fare. Lunch, dinner. $

Sun Spot
Makanda by the Sea Hotel, Quepos
Tel: 777-0442
Mediterranean cuisine plus fine selection of salads and seafood. $$–$$$

Volcán Arenal

Choza de Laurel
La Fortuna (behind the church)
Self-service, friendly atmosphere. $

Left: informal café society

NIGHTLIFE

If you want to sample the country's nightlife scene, you should head for the Central Valley region. Here you should not have any trouble finding all of the following: nightclubs at which the Latin dancing is so wild it might offend an Anglo-Saxon sensibility; cool and sophisticated bars featuring talented jazz pianists; and political hangouts with Latin *Nueva Trova* (protest) music.

There are also lots of opportunities to attend performances by local bands of all descriptions, classical-music orchestras and ensembles, dance companies, little theater groups, and internationally acclaimed artists. You can try your hand at blackjack and other gambling pursuits at a range of casinos that extends from fancy, five-star affairs to earthier, funky joints.

The best way to bring yourself up to date with what's happening during your visit is to check the 'What's Doing' section of the weekly *Tico Times*. You might want to make a point of seeing the bulletin board of the Teatro Nacional for upcoming events – an impressive array of national and international artists, including the Costa Rican National Symphony Orchestra, perform here. Teatro Melico Salazar, just west of the Teatro Nacional on Avenida 2, presents excellent, varied programs, including a large number of highly recommended dance performances.

Don't forget, if you are out in San José after dark, that for safety reasons you should use taxis rather than walk.

Listed on the following pages are some recommended bars, nightclubs, and other venues for a good night out.

Bars

Costa Rican bars often serve *bocas* (snacks) with your drink.

San José
Castro's Bar
Barrio México
Open every night of the week; bar until 11pm; disco until 5am. Atracts an after-work crowd. Latin music. *Bocas* served. Dance hall with DJs.

La Esmeralda
San José, Avenida 2, Calles 5–7
Mariachis stroll between the tables while they are waiting to play more formal gigs. Open late until after 4am.

La Villa
San Pedro *(near the university)*
Latin *Nueva Trova* music.

The Pub at the Corobicí
Corobicí Hotel
Tel: 239-0033
Popular venue frequently featuring live piano music.

Above: boogie night in San José

Shakespeare Bar
Paseo Colón area
Popular with an international crowd, the Shakespeare Bar has a darts board and often features jazz pianists, with combos also making occasional appearances.

Heredia
La Puerta de Alcalá
Lively and very popular. Cuban *Nueva Trova* (protest) music performed by local groups.

Escazú
Mac's American Bar
Darts and good times in a party atmosphere. Patronized by gringos and Tica yuppies. Good breakfasts.

Paladius
Plaza Colonial
Youthful clientele.

Casinos
Most of the country's larger hotels have a casino among their facilities. One of the best known casinos in San José is the one in Hotel San José Palacio (tel: 220-2034). Smaller than those in most of the other hotels, it offers a more intimate experience.

Concerts
Check the What's Doing section in the *Tico Times* for a complete listing of concerts and musical events throughout the Central Valley.

The Teatro Nacional hosts national and international artists, and concerts by the National Symphony (Apr–Nov).

Gay/Lesbian Spots
San José
La Avispa
Calle 1, Avenidas 8–10
Tel: 223-5343
Fax: 222-5913
Lesbian bar, but men welcome, too. Salsa Merengue. Three dance floors, pool tables, and a big-screen TV.

Déjá Vu
Calle 2, Avenidas 14–16
This is predominantly male, but women are also welcome. Offers cabaret, pop music, and dancing.

Movies
The following three large, modern cinema complexes in the Central Valley area have excellent projection and sound systems. They usually screen major American movies, with Spanish subtitles, three to six months after their US release dates.
San Pedro Mall
San Pedro
Tel: 283-5716

Plaza Colonial
San Rafael de Escazú
Tel: 289-9000

Real Mall Cariari
General Cañas Highway.

The following two, neighboring, movie theaters in San José screen non-Hollywood movies. See the *Tico Times* for subtitle details.
Sala Garbo
Avenida 2, Calle 28, San José
Tel: 222-1034

Left: the man with sax appeal
Above: the sign of good music

Teatro Laurence Olivier
Avenida 2, Calle 28,
San José
Tel: 222-1034

Nightclubs and Dancing

Ticos virtually always dress up when they go out to dance, and the time-honored, somewhat conservative tradition of dancing with a particular partner is still observed here. Women who go to clubs alone or in all-female groups should be prepared for a lot of male attention. Women very rarely invite men to dance.

The following list recommends a few old-time Costa Rican clubs where the emphasis is strictly on Latin music and dance (though the decor might suggest otherwise). There are also some upscale 'international' clubs, which feature a variety of music.

San José
Centro Comerical El Pueblo
Close to Villa Turnon on the highway to Heredia
There is something for everyone at this remarkable venue – a large complex full of boutiques, galleries, restaurants, nightclubs, bars, discos, and a skating rink. The highly eclectic musical offerings range from jazz and Latin fusion to Argentinian tango and Andean music (featuring lots of pan pipes). Discos here include **Cocloco**, **Infinito**, and the luxurious **La Plaza**.

El Cuartel de
la Boca del Monte
Avenida 1, Calles 21–23, San José
Tel: 221-0327
A popular singles bar, providing live music at weekends. Situated Downtown, near Cine California.

San Rafael Arriba
Típico Los Higuerones
Hard-core Latino dancing. Live music and a full restaurant.

Heredia
Tica Linda
Big dance floor. DJs and occasional live bands perform on weekends. Music includes Latin salsa and rock.

Ezcazú
Baabú
Trejos Montealegre de Escazú
This club attracts a wide range of age groups, and features live bands and DJs every night of the week.

Pool Halls

Escazú's Plaza Colonial has an excellent pool hall, with lots of tables available to players of all levels. Pool halls in Costa Rica do not necessarily share the somewhat insalubrious reputation of their counterparts in some other countries.

Theater

San José has a lively theater scene and you will usually find one or two plays being performed in English, in addition to the various Spanish-language options. To find out what's on while you are in town, check the listings in the *Tico Times* .

Dance

Costa Rica's dance scene is one of the best in the world. The Central American dance aesthetic is a spectacular one – you might want to attend a performace even if you are not a dance aficionado. The **National Dance Company** performs classical and modern works, some by Costa Rican or Central American choreographers.

The **Teatro Melico Salazar** company in San José stages productions several times a month; the company also performs at the **Teatro Nacional**. Tickets for performances are relatively inexpensive.

To view authentic Costa Rican dance in a more relaxed setting, traditional top-quality dancing and singing can be seen at the **Fantasía Folklórica** in the Melico Salazar every Tuesday.

Right: a girls' night out

SPORTS AND ACTIVITIES

Costa Rica offers some of the most varied and exciting adventure and sport activities in Central America, ranging from trekking, mountain-biking, motor-cycle tours, horse-back riding, and golf to world-class surfing, wind-surfing, and whitewater rafting. There are many excellent tour operators who can put together a multi-activity itinerary covering different parts of the country.

Fans of adventure sports should check out www.bungee.co.cr for information on bungee jumping, paragliding and climbing

Cycling

Although the major roads are often steep and potholed and local drivers are generally inconsiderate to cyclists, mountain-biking is increasingly popular and it is possible to arrange tours lasting from a day to a week or rent a bicycle at one of the lodges and beach resorts. The area around La Fortuna and Lake Arenal is excellent with plenty of trails, and good accommodations.

Aguas Bravas
PO Box 1504-2100
Tel: 292 2072
website: www.aguas-bravas.co.cr
A wide range of tours.
Coast to Coast Adventures
Apdo 2135-1002 San José
Tel: 225 6055
website: www.ctoadventures.com
Good selection of itineraries and activities.

Rock River Lodge
Arenal
Tel: 695-5644
Email: rokriver@solracsa.co.cr
A cozy lodge that is popular with adventure travelers. Owner Norman List is a dedicated mountain-biker and windsurfer and offers good advice as well as renting out equipment.

Motorcycling

A few companies offer self-guided and accompanied motorcycling tours of the country. Riders need to be at least 25 and experienced:

Rent-a-Harley Davidson & Tours
Tel: 289-5552
Website: www.arweb.com/harleytours
Can arrange tours and rentals lasting from oen to 10 days.
Road Runner Motor Expedition
(part of Costa Rica Trails)
Tel: 221 3011
Website: www.roadrunnermoto.com
Offers BMW tours throughout Costa Rica and Central America.

Canopy Tours

There are now many ways to experience the canopy life of the rain and cloud forests of Costa Rica, ranging from simple tree platforms to a ride on a modified ski-lift that takes visitors floating through the tree tops, or the more adventurous tours which entail strapping on a climbing harness and gliding along cables suspended over the canopy. There are new spin-off canopy tour companies and it is always recommended that you check out safety conditions and how the tour operates before making a reservation.
Aerial Tram
Tel: 257-5961
Website: www.rainforesttram.com
Only 50 minutes from San José. One of the safest ways to experience the rain forest.
Canopy Tours
Tel: 256-7626
Website: www.canopytour.co.cr
Has sites in Aguas Zarcas, Igunap Rark, Rincón de la Vieja, and Monteverde, where the original canopy tour was developed. The tour starts with a climb up a rope ladder through a strangler fig tree. There are three platforms and two traverses. Not recommended if you suffer from

Left: all set for a canopy tour
Right: rodeo riders

vertigo, but a unique way of experiencing and supporting the rainforest. Reservations are often necessary in the high season.

Sky Walk
Monteverde
Tel: 645-5238
A new and tranquil option, comprising a walk along forest trails and over five suspension bridges high above the cloud forest.

Fishing

Costa Rica's rich marine life is an angler's dream come true. Along the Pacific Coast anglers find some of the best blue water and inshore fishing in the world, with abundant sailfish, billfish, and marlin, while the canals and rivers of the northern Atlantic coast feature world-class snook and tarpon fishing. There is also good freshwater fishing in Lake Arenal and trout fishing in mountain streams. Although Lake Arenal has a closed season from October through December, the ocean is always open. It is generally agreed that the Pacific Coast is slowest from September through November while the Caribbean is slower in June and July.

A catch and release policy operates to protect the excellent fishing reserves, and a fishing license is required, normally organized by the guide. They can also be obtained at the Banco Credito Agricola on Avenida 4, between Calle Central and Calle 1 in San José. Freshwater permits are cheap but deep sea fishing permits are much more expensive and some visitors can pay up to $1,000 a day for world-class fishing. Good sources of information on fishing in Costa Rica are:

Americana Fishing Services, tel: 223-4331, email: fishing@sol.racsa.co.cr
Carlos Barrantes, La Casa del Pescador, tackle shop at Calle 2, Avenidas 18–20, San José.

Golf

Golf continues to grow in popularity in Costa Rica. The best golf-course is the 18-hole championship course at the **Cariari Country Club** (tel: 239-2455) and guests staying at the **Melia Cariari** (tel: 239-0022) can occasionally use the course. There is also an 18- hole course at the **Melia Playa Conchal** in Guanacaste (tel: 654-4123) and a par-72 Ted Robinson-designed golf course at the **Marriott Los Suenos Resort** at Playa Herradura (tel: 630-9000), website: www.marriott.com

Hiking

Costa Rica's National Parks are ideal for trekking. Hikes can range from short nature trails in the rain forest to treks staggered over several days, perhaps combined with mountaineering in some of the remoter mountainous areas.

Areas particularly popular with hikers include Monteverde, Rincón de la Vieja National Park, Corcovado National Park, and Chirripó National Park. There is also a good slection of well-marked hiking trails in the country's growing number of private reserves.

Horse-riding

Part of Costa Rican culture, horseback-riding is still a major part of rural life. It is easy to

rent horses to explore beaches, country roads, and forest trails, although a little equestrian experience is useful as *ticos* use different saddles, stirrups, and neck-rein steering. Many resort and tourist areas offer short rides or even overnight trips, but be aware that there are some unscrupulous companies that overwork their horses, especially in the Fortuna-Monteverde area, and that the lowest-price tour is not necessarily the best.

Recommended companies include:

Coast to Coast Adventures
Tel: 225-6055
Website: www.ctoadventures.com
Costa Rican Adventure Travel
Quepos
Tel: 777-1170
Has an interesting tour through the virgin rainforest of the Rain Maker reserve.
Rancho Savegre Horseback Tours
Quepos
Tel: 777-0528.

Scuba diving and Snorkeling

Costa Rica's underwater wonders range from coastal reefs to offshore islands with diverse marine life such as giant manta rays, sea turtles, moray eels, white-tipped sharks, colorful coral gardens, and smaller tropical fish. Visibility depends on the season and location and is often adequate but seldom crystal-clear. The country's largest coastal reef is protected within Cahuita National Park on the Caribbean coast, where it is easy to rent snorkeling equipment and boats. There are other good places to dive between Puerto Viejo and Manzanillo, with the best visibility from March through early May and from mid-August through mid-November. However, the Pacific has the best diving, with less coral but plenty of big fish.

In the northwest there are dive centers at Playa del Coco, Ocotal, and Hermosa, where it is possible to learn to dive and rent equipment. Conditions are generally best from June through September.

Farther south it is possible to arrange dive trips from Drakes Bay to the reefs near Caño Island, where there are huge schools of fish, rocky corals, and undersea canyons. Experienced divers can make the 36-hour journey by sea to Cocos Island, touted by Jacques Cousteau as one of the finest deep-water dive sites in the world.

Some recommended companies include:

Bill Beard's Diving Safaris
Playa Hermosa
Tel: 670-0012
Email: costarica@diveres.com
Website: www.billbeardcostarica.com
Possibly the best diving operation in the country. Also offers Nitrox courses, dives, and adventure tours.
Diving Safaris
Hotel El Ocotal
Tel: 670-0321
Email: elocotal@sol.racsa.co.cr
One of the longest-established dive shops in the country, which can organize groups, expeditions, and certification courses.

Cocos Travel
Tel: 290-6737
Website: www.divecocos.com
Specializes in dive trips to Cocos and operates *Sea Hunter* and *Undersea Hunter*. Costs approximately $3,000 for a 10-day tour from San José.

Swimming and Surfing

There is good swimming and surfing on both the Caribbean and Pacific coasts, although some beaches may not be suitable all year round. Dangers for swimmers include rip tides and large waves, caused by heavy swells, that may hit you unexpectedly as you leave the water. Sharks may also be present. Always ask for advice from locals before entering the sea. Many surfers bring their own board to Costa Rica and rent jeeps to travel around more easily.

Among the best surfing beaches on the Pacific Coast include Naranjo, Tamarindo, Jacó, Hermosa, Quepos, Dominical, and Pavones. On the Caribbean Coast, try Puerto Viejo and Punta Uva.

For up-to-date information regarding surfing conditions, call the 24-hour **Costa Rican Surf Report Hotline**, tel: 233-7386 or visit www.crsurf.com. Good general information on surfing can also be found on the website www.surf-the-earth.com.

Whitewater Rafting & Kayaking

Costa Rica's mountainous topography and copious rainfall make it one of the most popular locations in the world for whitewater river running, whether a first-time rafter or a world-class kayaker. There is an enormous variety of wilderness experiences ranging from gentle family float trips through luscious landscapes with abundant wildlife to exhilarating rapids.

Only a short drive from San José, the Reventazón is Costa Rica's best known river, and companies *(see below)* offer a variety of day-trips and longer tours throughout the year to suit paddlers of all levels of ability.

For experienced rafters, the Pacuare is deemed to be the most challenging river, passing through lush gorges toward the Caribbean. Other popular options are the gentle Corobici for bird-watching, the Sarapiqui, and the Pascua.

The main companies specialising in whitewater rafting are:

Costa Rica Expeditions
Tel: 257-0766
Website www.costaricaexpeditions.com
The original rafting company, with an excellent reputation.

Rios Tropicales
Tel: 233-6455
Website: www.riostropicales.com
Has a variety of rafting and kayaking trips and is owned and operated by Costa Rican kayaking champions.

Aventuras Naturales
Tel: 225-3939
Website: www.toenjoynature.com
The third main player. Runs the popular Pacuare Jungle Lodge.

Windsurfing

Lake Arenal is considered one of the three best places in the world to windsurf and serious windsurfers come between December and April. This period isn't recommended for beginniers, as trade winds blow too strongly, but during the rest of the year, Lake Arenal is an ideal place to learn, and it is possible to arrange instruction and rental at the **Hotel Tilawa** (tel: 695-5050, email: tilawa@solracsa.co.cr).

Left: still waters on the Nicoya Peninsula
Above: back on dry land

CALENDAR OF EVENTS

Festivals, fiestas, and parades in Costa Rica are often exhilarating, outrageous, and sometimes even slightly alarming to visitors accustomed to more orderly and controlled public events. The huge crowds swell to unbelievable proportions, the noise rises, the excitement grows, and yet everything seems to proceed in a most peaceable way. Festivals honoring the patron saints of villages and towns are often announced by unexpected volleys of gunshots, and the loud music and festivities continue long into the night. At Costa Rican bullfights, young men simply jump into the ring to tease the bull and demonstrate their daring, while a Red Cross van stands on the sidelines in readiness. At even the largest parades, there doesn't seem to be anyone directing the traffic or restraining the crowds.

For details of all special events, festivals, and performances, consult the weekly English-language newspapers such as the *Tico Times* or *Costa Rica Today*.

January

Festivities inaugurating the **New Year** conclude with a parade of horses and riders *(El Tope)* down Paseo Colón in downtown San José, usually on Jan 2. Central Valley horses, from humble working steeds to elegant *paso finos*, are on parade.

The **Copa del Café** is a week-long tennis tournament in San José for the best junior players from around the world.

February

La Fiesta de los Diabolitos (The Festival of the Little Devils) is an allegorical re-creation of the struggle between the native people (Borucas) and the Spanish. It takes place in the native village of Rey Curré, in the southern zone.

March

This is the time of year when hundreds of species of orchid blossom. Some 800 species can be seen at Lankester Gardens *(see page 30)*, some 7km (5 miles) southeast of Cartago. The **National Orchid Show** takes place in San José. For more information, write to the Orchid Association of Costa Rica, Apdo 6351,1000 San José, Costa Rica.

The **National Symphony Season** begins at the historic Teatro Nacional in March. Performances are held in the evenings and on Sunday afternoons.

Día de Boyero, the Day of the Oxcart Driver, is celebrated in San Antonio de Escazú in mid-March. Pairs of giant oxen pulling brightly painted carts are brought to the church to be blessed.

Some 1,000 people run in **La Carrera de la Paz**, a race from the Gymnasium to the University for Peace in Ciudad Colón.

Above: a local amateur tries his hand at bullfighting; not an advisable pursuit for visitors

The **Bonanza Cattle Show** takes place at the Bonanza Fairgrounds, just outside the city limits of San José. The event includes Costa Rican-style bullfights, rodeos, and horse races.

Hundreds of artisans display their wares at a giant **crafts fair** held for one week in the Plaza de la Cultura in downtown San José. Consult the *Tico Times* for dates, which vary from year to year.

The **International Festival of the Arts** attracts artists of all types from all over the world for 11 days of performances held at the Teatro Nacional, La Plaza de la Cultura, and at other locations.

April–May

During the course of **Easter Week** *(Semana Santa)* many businesses and government offices are closed, and *Josefinos* (residents of San José) take off for vacations at the beaches and in the countryside. Any number of elaborate religious processions take pride of place in cities and villages throughout the country, including San Antonio de Escazú, San Isidro de Heredia, Santo Domingo de Heredia, and Cartago.

La Carrera de San Juan, the country's biggest annual marathon, usually attracts more than 1,000 competitors, who run the 42.195km (26 miles) from El Alto de Ocho-mongo near Cartago to San Juan de Tibás, north of San José.

July

The **Mango Festival** in Alajuela features parades, music, food, and crafts.

The anniversary of the **Annexation of Guanacaste**, on July 25, is celebrated with fiestas, parades, bullfights, and rodeos in Liberia and Santa Cruz in the province of Guanacaste.

This is the month when turtles start nesting on the beaches of Tortuguero.

August 1 & 2

Thousands of the faithful make a **pilgrimage** from San José to Cartago in honor of the country's patron saint, the **Virgen de Los Ángeles**. A statue of the Black Virgin (known as *La Negrita*) miraculously appeared in the forest where Cartago's basilica now stands. Many miracles are attributed to the beloved Virgin, as the result of which her shrine is full of offerings from petitioners whose prayers she has answered.

Turtles continue to dig nests on the beaches of Tortuguero.

September–October

September 15 is Costa Rica's **Independence Day**. Parades featuring marching bands take place throughout the country. At 6pm traffic throughout the country comes to a halt and everyone sings the national anthem.

October 12, **Columbus Day** (or El Día de las Culturas, as it is now called), is the occasion of a week-long carnival in Puerto Limón. The highlight of Carnival Week is the parade, when thousands take to the streets to join in a great spectacle of music and dance.

On the beaches of Guanacaste and Tortuguero, the turtles approach the end of their nesting season.

December

During the week between Christmas and New Year, there is a nightly **carnival** at the fairground in Zapote. It features fairground rides, special carnival food, and Costa Rican-style bullfights, at which amateur and aspiring professional matadors jump into the bullring to harass the bulls. Although it is said that the bulls are never physically harmed, the young men sometimes do themselves considerable damage.

Right: supplicants at Cartago

Practical Information

GETTING THERE

By Air
Although some international flights to Costa Rica now arrive at Daniel Oduber/Tomas Guardia Airport in Liberia (Guanacaste Province), most still land at Juan Santamaría International Airport, a 20-minute drive from San José. A cab ride to your Central Valley hotel should cost around $12–20. If there is no meter in the cab, agree on the fare before committing yourself. The bus fare into town is very cheap.

Make reservations for your flight as far ahead as possible, especially if you plan to travel between December and February or at Easter. Ask for your confirmation number. It is best to confirm your reservation 72 hours before departure and arrive at the airport at least two hours in advance.

Airport Tax
There is an exit tax ($17 at the time of going to press) for departing tourists. This is not usually included in the price of your air ticket.

By Road
The Interamerican Highway allows for fairly rapid transit into Costa Rica. If you take a vehicle into the country, it will be noted on your passport. Leaving the country without the vehicle, once it has been noted, can be problematic. It may be necessary to show the border authorities that you have a sufficient supply of cash for your stay.

Tica Bus (tel: 221-8954; fax 221-9229) provides a comfortable and reliable bus service throughout Central America. There is a daily bus service from Nicaragua and Panamá to Costa Rica.

By Sea
Cruise ships arrive at Puerto Limón, on the Atlantic Coast, and at Puerto Caldera, on the Pacific. Check with a travel agent to find out which cruise lines sail to Costa Rica.

Puntarenas, on the Pacific coast, has a well-managed yacht club, which is one of the first stops for transoceanic yachts from Western USA ports of call.

TRAVEL ESSENTIALS

When to Visit
In the Central Valley, the dry season generally lasts from December through April. This is the high season, especially between Christmas and New Year, and during the Easter holiday, when it can be extremely difficult to reserve airline tickets, lodgings, or rental cars.

The rainy season is between May and November, when most mornings are bright and sunny but afternoons often bring rain. The vegetation is green and fresh, and "green season" discounts are often available at hotels. November is an ideal time to visit, when the rains are subsiding but the high season is not in full swing. On the Caribbean Coast, however, rain can fall at any time.

Visas and Passports
Citizens of Canada, Great Britain, the USA, and many European countries are given 90-day visas on entering Costa Rica. Citizens of other countries are usually given 30-day visas. Visa extensions are possible, but are much more easily obtained through your travel agent. Check on the latest regulations before leaving home.

Visitors must have at pre-paid airline ticket to another country in order to enter Costa Rica.

Left: slowly does it
Right: cruising Costa Rican-style

Always carry your passport with you (or, for safety, a photocopy), and report any lost ID immediately.

For further information, contact the Embassy of Costa Rica, Washington, DC 20009, or the Costa Rican Tourist Institute (Instituto Costarricense de Turismo), Apdo 777-1000, San José, Costa Rica, tel/fax: (506) 223-1733; toll free telephone number from the USA 1-800 343 6332; website: www.tourism-costarica.com.

In San José, UK citizens can contact the British Embassy at Edificio Centro Colon, 11th floor, Paseo Colon, Calles 38 and 40, tel: 258-2025, fax: 233-9938. The US Embassy is situated in front of Centro Comercial on Carretera Pavas, tel: 220-3939, fax: 220-2305.

Vaccinations

No vaccinations are required in order to be able to visit Costa Rica. Malaria is not a problem here, except in remote regions of Talamanca. Cholera is not generally a problem either, but away from hotels and restaurants it is perhaps wise to avoid ice and unpeeled fruit. There have been instances of dengue fever which is carried by mosquitoes – take adequate precautions to avoid being bitten, especially in lowland urban areas such as Liberia and Puerto Limón.

Customs

Travelers are usually waved through customs or given only a cursory check, unless carrying excessive baggage. A maximum of six rolls of film, 500 grams (18 oz) of tobacco, 2kg (4.4 lbs) of candy, and 3 liters (5.28 pints) of wine or liquor (for travelers aged over 21) can be brought in to the country.

Prescription drugs should be kept in their original containers. Costa Rica is serious about curtailing the flow of illegal drugs. Don't risk carrying them.

Weather

The average temperature in San José and environs is about 24°C (75°F). In the highlands, temperatures drop around 10° for every 150 meters (500 ft) of elevation. Temperatures along the coasts range from around 25°C (70°F) to 30°C plus (90°F), usually with high humidity.

Clothing

Bring clothes and shoes suitable for the activities you plan to undertake (beach-going, hiking, rafting, horseback riding, etc.) as well as smarter clothes for San José restaurants and nightlife.

Costa Ricans tend to dress rather more formally than most Europeans and North Americans. Shorts are worn for sports and at the beach, but never in cities. Sweaters and jackets are needed for cool evenings and in the mountains.

Bring rain-gear and shoes that are suitable for muddy trails if you plan to hike. A sun-hat and umbrella are also useful, and it is a good idea to bring insect repellent, medications, sunscreen, tampons and contraceptives with you as they can be expensive and difficult to purchase outside San José.

Electricity

Electricity runs at 110 volts AC, 60Hz, and sockets are made for two-prong flat and round plugs. American and Canadian appliances, whose plugs do not have grounding prongs, will usually work here.

Time Differences

GMT minus six hours. The same as Central Time in the USA.

GETTING ACQUAINTED

Geography

Costa Rica is located near the center of the Central American isthmus, with Nicaragua to the north, and Panamá to the south. To the east is the Atlantic Ocean, with beautiful Caribbean beaches, and to the west are hundreds of kilometers of Pacific coastline.

It is a small country, one of the smallest in Latin America, covering less than 20,000 sq miles (52,000 sq km). There are steamy coastal plains and beaches of every description, high mountains, unmapped virgin rainforests, cloud forests, tropical dry forests, jungles, mangrove swamps, plains and pastures, and active volcanoes.

The diversity of animal life matches the diversity of landscapes: there are more than 850 species of birds; around 130 species of freshwater fish; 208 species of mammals,

including big cats; approximately 1,000 species of butterflies; and hundreds of thousands of species of insects.

Government and Economy

Costa Rica is a democracy governed by a president, two vice-presidents, and a legislative assembly. Elections are held every four years. The Constitution, adopted in 1949 after a civil war, abolished the military. Costa Rica has one of the highest living standards in the southern hemisphere, free public health care and education, and one of the highest literacy rates (92 percent) in Central, South, or North America.

Tourism, bananas, and coffee are Costa Rica's top three national products, with microchips, textiles, and medical instruments making up an increasingly important part of the country's economy.

Religion

The majority of Costa Ricans are Catholic (70 percent), although Protestant Evangelical religions are becoming increasingly popular. There is a small Jewish community in San José, and a small community of Friends (Quakers) in Monteverde.

How Not to Offend

Costa Ricans tend to be quite formal, reserved, and polite. Spanish speakers will be interested to note that the informal *tu* is almost never used. An archaic form, *vos* (the rules of which elude even advanced students

of Spanish) is used within the family and between good friends. To avoid confusion, however, it is best to stick with *usted*, which is always correct. The best way to get along in Costa Rica is to be friendly, polite, and calm. Avoid raising one's voice, getting angry, or causing another to "lose face".

Population (Ethnicity)

Racially, the population of Costa Rica is rather complex. About 1 percent of the population are *indigenas* or native inhabitants. Costa Ricans of the Central Valley are predominantly of Spanish descent. They speak Spanish, and proudly refer to themselves as *Ticos*. The people of Guanacaste, many of whom are descended from the Chorotega Indians, resemble their Nicaraguan neighbors in manner and accent, and call themselves *Guanacastecos*.

Black Costa Ricans *(Negros)* of the Caribbean Coast region, whose ancestors were Jamaican workers who came to Costa Rica to fish or work on the Atlantic Railroad, speak English and Spanish. There are also many Chinese Costa Ricans *(Chinos),* whose forebears also came to construct the railroad. The native people of Costa Rica *(Indígenas)* live in the more remote areas of the country, often on reserves.

The most recently arrived immigrant groups in Costa Rica are the Europeans and North Americans *(Gringos),* and political and economic refugees *(Nicas)* from Nicaragua.

Above: a rich ethnic mix

MONEY MATTERS

Currency
The unit of currency is the *colón*. Money can be changed at the airport until 5pm.

Money Changers
The service in national banks is notoriously slow, and having to waiting in line for an infuriating two hours to change money is not uncommon. Money-exchange houses, called *casas de cambio*, provide a more efficient service. Ask at your hotel; they may change money for you or will refer you to a *casa de cambio*.

National banks are open weekdays, 9am–3pm; private banks open 8am–3.30pm. The current rate of exchange can be found in the daily newspaper, and the English-language weeklies.

Change *colone*s back into dollars before departing from Costa Rica. The airport bank will cash only $50 worth of *colone*s for departing travelers.

It is advisable to travel with travelers' checks and cash in small denominations. You may not be able to break 5,000 *colón* notes when paying for taxis and other services, so bear this in mind. It is increasingly easy to find ATMs (cash machines) in shopping centers and offices, but beware, as there may be hidden charges.

Black Markets
It is illegal to change money on the streets, although the government often turn a blind eye to the practice. In addition, tourists changing money in this way are often cheated on the rate of exchange.

Above: negotiating a fare
Right: flying over Central Valley

Credit Cards
American Express, Visa, and Mastercard are widely accepted at restaurants and hotels in the Central Valley, but if you travel to the beaches or the mountains you will probably need cash or travelers' checks, except at large hotels. It is common for hotels and other tourist establishments to add a 7–8 percent surcharge to purchases with credit cards. Check before using your card.

If your card is lost or stolen you can call the following numbers:
American Express: 257-0155
Diners Club: 257-2351
MasterCard: 257-4744
Visa: 257-4744

Tipping
Restaurants add a 10 percent gratuity to your check, but it's customary to leave an additional tip of perhaps 5 percent, if the service warrants it. Hotel bellboys, maids, and tour guides should also be tipped.

Taxes
Hotels and restaurants add a 13 percent sales tax to your bill and 10 percent service charge. Hotels also add a 3.45 percent tourism tax on room charges.

GETTING AROUND

Domestic Flights
Domestic flights are fairly inexpensive and can provide a comfortable alternative to many hours on bad roads. Sansa and Travelair (recommended) serve many destinations. Domestic flights fly into Juan SantaMaria Airport (Sansa) or Tobias Bolaños Airport in Pavas. It is also possible to charter flights, and to book helicopter tours.

Aero Costa Sol, tel: 296-1111; fax: 441-2671. Charter flights.

Heli Tours, tel: 220-3940; fax 290-3044; e-mail: fly@heli-tour.com. Company running helicopter tours.

Sansa, tel: 221-9414 fax: 255-2176.

Travelair, tel: 220-3054; fax: 220-0413; email: Travelair@centralamerica.com.

Taxis

Licensed taxis are red with a taxi sign on the roof. They are widely used and inexpensive – fares within San José are generally just a few dollars. All taxis are supposed to have working meters *(marías)*. If your driver has no *maría*, negotiate the fare before getting in, or find a taxi whose *maría* is working.

Buses

You can travel anywhere in Costa Rica by bus. Consider taking at least one bus trip during your visit, if only to a nearby Central Valley town, as it is a good way to experience local life.

The main bus stop in the center of San José is the Coca-Cola terminal, at Calle 16, Ave 1–3. The Costa Rican Tourist Institute (ICT) office, below Plaza de la Cultura, has a list of bus companies' names and telephone numbers (tel: 223-1733). The weekly English- and Spanish-language newspaper, *Costa Rica Today*, often carries a page of current bus information.

Rental Cars

Rental cars are not recommended for getting around San José, but make sense for trips outside the city, though driving conditions in Costa Rica can be quite trying. Consider using public transportation or a paid driver for your first day or two, before you decide whether you wish to take on the task of driving yourself.

Car rental rates are generally around $40–60 per day, including insurance. Four-wheel drive vehicles (recommended for many areas outside the Central Valley, especially during the rainy season) are twice the price of an ordinary car.

Reserve your vehicle as far in advance as possible. Pre-payment is advised, especially during the high season (Dec–Feb) and during the Easter holdiay. Among the better car rental companies are: Alamo, tel: 233-7733; Dollar, tel: 222-8920; Elegante, one of the few which offers non-deductible insurance, tel: 221-0066; Toyota, tel: 223-2250; and Adobe Rent A Car, tel: 258-4242, email: info@adobecar.com.

For general car rental information, email: travel@informatica.co.cr

Driving in Costa Rica

In the past two years, the government has invested heavily in improving the roads, but some are still in poor condition. Drivers weave all over the road to avoid the sometimes enormous potholes *(huecos)* and so will you, after you've hit a few. In addition, in the wet season months of June through November, the roads can be prone to landslides and floods. Two main-beam blinks usually indicate that the other driver is allowing you the right-of-way.

If you are waved over by the police, pull over. Don't try to drive away, as they will simply radio ahead to have you stopped. Be sure to have all automobile documents in the car, and be polite.

It is illegal for police to demand on-the-spot payment of fines for traffic violation or to solicit a bribe. Wear your seatbelt and observe the speed limits (radar is often used on the highways).

Don't drive without insurance and a valid driver's license. If you are in an accident, don't move your vehicle until the police come, otherwise it will be assumed that you are the guilty party.

In the cities, park in one of the inexpensive, attended parking lots *(parqueos)*. Avoid parking illegally, as violators' cars are sometimes towed away. Always lock your vehicle, and never leave any valuables inside.

Private Tour Drivers

Hiring a skilled, English-speaking driver, experienced with Costa Rican roads, is a good way to become familiar with driving conditions and a much more relaxing way of getting to your destination. We highly recommend the services of Carlos Mora (tel: 232-9870/384-4576), a delightful man who speaks excellent English and is a very good driver. Alternatively, call the ICT (Costa Rican Tourism Institute), tel: 223-1733, or contact a reputable local tour operator to book a car with driver.

Ferries

Puntarenas to Playa Naranjo: departs 5.10am, 8.50am, and 12.50pm.

Playa Naranjo to Puntarenas: departs 3.15am, 7am, and 10.50am. For further information, tel: 661-3834, fax: 661-2197, website: www.asstcard.co.cr/guia/homp/ferryn.htm.

Puntarenas to Paquera: departs 7.30am, noon, and 5pm.

Paquera to Puntarenas: departs 6am, 11am, and 3.15am.

Tempisque River: from 6am–7pm, every 20 minutes.

HOURS AND HOLIDAYS

Business Hours

Business hours are generally Monday to Friday, 9am–5pm, with a two-hour lunch break from noon–2pm. National banks are usually open from 9am–3pm on weekdays with some staying open until 7pm in San José; private banks are open from 8am and close anytime between 3.30 and 5pm, depending on the bank. Stores are generally open Mon–Sat 8am–7pm. Some shopping malls are open on Sundays and in the evenings.

Public Holidays and Festivals

January 1: New Year's Day.

Mid-January: Fiesta de Santa Cruz (Nicoya Peninsula), rodeos, bullfights, music, and dancing.

March 19: Feast of St Joseph (patron saint of San José).

April 11: Anniversary of Battle of Rivas.

Holy Thursday to Easter Sunday

May 1: Labor Day.

June (Thursday after Trinity Sunday): Corpus Christi.

June (third Sunday): Father's Day.

June 29: Feast of St Peter and St Paul.

July 25: Annexation of Guanacaste Province.

August 2: Feast of Our Lady of the Angels (patron saint of Costa Rica).

August 15: Assumption of the Blessed Virgin; also Mother's Day.

September 15: Independence Day.

October 12: Columbus Day, now called El Día de las Culturas.

Mid-October: a week-long Carnival held in Puerto Limón.

December 24–25: Christmas Eve and Christmas Day.

Government and business offices, including banks and post offices, are virtually closed down from Christmas to the New Year and in the latter part of Easter week (*Semana Santa*). Generally, buses do not run from Thursday through Sunday of Easter week, so make sure you have other means of transportation during this period.

Market Days

Saturday morning is market day in Escazú and Heredia, as well as in many small towns. A huge variety of local fruit and vegetables, as well as fresh flowers, honey, and baked goods are sold.

ACCOMMODATIONS

It is advisable to book ahead if you want to stay in any of the big luxury hotels, especially during high season and at Christmas or Easter. A sales tax of 13 percent and a tourism tax of 3.39 percent are added to all accommodation bills. Price brackets, which

Left: market day

are based on two people sharing a double room, are as follows:

$$$$	$100–300
$$$	$70–90
$$	$40–70
$	$20–40

San José/Central Valley

There is a wide choice of accommodation in downtown San José and its surrounding sub-urbs, ranging from budget backpackers' hostels to charming inns. Those visitors with only a short time in San José may prefer to stay downtown in one of the renovated older houses, but many visitors prefer to stay in one of the suburbs such as Escazú which is only 15 minutes west of the city and has wonderful views of the Central Valley.

Downtown
Hotel Grano de Oro
Calle 30, Avenidas 2–4
Tel: 255-3322; Fax: 221-2782
Email: granoro@sol.racsa.co.cr
Charming converted 19th-century mansion with pretty courtyards and fountains, excellent garden restaurant and 35 unique rooms and suites. Quiet location and panoramic views of the city, plus excellent service. Early booking recommended. $$$

Fleur de Lys Hotel
Calle 13, Avenidas 2 & 6
Tel: 233-1206; Fax: 257-3637
Email: florlys@sol.racsa.co.cr
Website: www.hotelfleurdelys.com
Located close to the National Museum of San José and only five-minutes' walk from downtown, this elegantly-restored mansion has 19 rooms individually decorated. The hotel restaurant is popular with locals. $$$

Escazú
Hotel Alta
Alto de las Palomas
Tel: 282-4160; Fax: 282-4162
Email: hotlalta@solracsa.co.cr
Website: www.altatravelplanners.com
Well worth the expense, this gem of a hotel lies 5 miles (8km) west of San José between Escazú and Santa Ana with spectacular views over the valley and city. Infused with colonial charm, the individually-designed guestrooms have custom-made furnishings and every modern convenience. Facilities include the excellent La Luz Restaurant, swimming pool and health spa. $$$$

Casa de las Tias
San Rafael de Escazú
Tel: 289-5517; Fax: 289-7353
Sprawling Victorian-style house set in lush gardens. Original Latin American art and private baths. $$–$$$

Posada el Quijote
Bello Horizonte de Escazú
Tel: 289-8401; Fax: 289-8729
Email: quijote@quijote.co.cr
This is a lovely country home, converted into a B&B adorned with a modern art collection and attractive gardens and offering panoramic views. $$

San Gildar
Between Escazú and Santa Ana on the old highway
Tel: 289-8843; Fax: 228-6454
Email: info@hotelsangildar.com
A pleasant luxury/business hotel with lush tropical gardens, pool, restaurant and bar. The third-floor rooms are generally the most quiet. $$$

Tara Resort Hotel & Spa
Singposted from Escazú
Tel: 228-6992; Fax: 228-9651
Email: tara@tararesort.com
Website: www.tararesort.com
A plantation-style mansion and spa that could have come straight out of *Gone With the Wind*. It offers heaps of southern grandeur and a spectacular setting overlooking the Central Valley. Wide variety of spa treatments available. Also has an excellent dining room. $$$$

Heredia and Airport Area
Finca Rosa Blanca Country Inn
Santa Bárbara de Heredia
Tel: 269-9392; Fax: 269-9555
Email: rblanca@sol.racsa.co.cr
An extraordinary small hotel in the foothills of Heredia. Romantic and fanciful with eclectic architecture and original art. $$$$

the Reventazón River at the base of the Turrialba Mountains. It has 16 elegant rooms and suites, a gourmet restaurant, spring-fed pool, jacuzzi, tennis, and putting. Good base for hiking, rafting, and tours to the pre-Columbian Guayabo ruins.

Parque Nacional Volcan Poás

Poás Volcano Lodge
16 km (10 miles) from Varablanca
Tel/fax: 482-2194
UK tel: 01420-549205
Email: Poasvl@solracsa.co.cr
Website: www.arweb.com./poas
This eco-lodge is set at an altitude of 1,900 metres (6,233ft), with stunning views over the northern Caribbean plains, the Atlantic coastline, and Poás Volcano. Warm and spacious accommodations, lovely main sitting area with sunken fireplace, billiard room, healthy cuisine, exuberant gardens, jungle trails, and many other outdoor activities, such as riding, cycling and whitewater rafting. Definitely the best lodge in the area. $$-$$$

The Caribbean Coast

Parque Nacional Tortuguero
If possible, visit Tortuguero either between February and July for the nesting season of the leatherback turtle or July through October for that of the green turtle. Most visitors spend at least two nights in the park, and a number of lodges provide comfortable accommodations, guides, boats, and family-style dining. Most of the lodges can be booked as part of an itinerary (including transportation) through one of the many San José operators or directly through the lodge itself. There are more basic places to stay in Tortuguero, costing approximately $8–20 per person but excluding meals, activities, and the services of a guide.

Laguna Lodge
Tortuguero
Tel: 225-3470; Fax: 283-8031
A small and cozy lodge on a narrow strip of land between the Caribbean Sea and the Tortuguero Lagoon, with free-form pool, rustic restaurant and hammock huts scat-

Marriott Hotel & Resort
San Antonio de Belen, five minutes from the airport
Tel: 298-0000; Fax: 298-0011
Email: costaric@marriott.co.cr
Attractive colonial-style resort located in a 30-acre coffee plantation with superb leisure facilities, including two swimming pools, golf, tennis, and health club plus a choice of excellent dining options. A good base for a longer stay in the San José area. $$$$

Xandari
Alajuela
Tel: 443-2020; Fax: 442-4847
Email: paradise@xandari.com
Website: www.xandari.com
A 15 minutes' drive from the airport and set in a peaceful coffee plantation on a ridge overlooking the Central Valley, this is a tiny hotel of striking architectural design comprsing 16 spacious suites and villas. Delicious breakfasts are served on a large terrace and main meals are served in the lodge. Two pools, a jacuzzi and an outdoor gym. $$$$

Turrialba

Casa Turire
Turrialba
Tel: 531-1111; Fax: 531-1075
Email: casaturire@ticonet.co.cr
Located 90 minutes' drive from San José, the colonial-style Casa Turire is the luxurious centerpiece of a spectacular coffee, macadamia nut and sugar cane plantation on the banks of

tered throughout the garden. There are 30 rooms with fans and private facilities. $$$

Mawamba Lodge
Tortuguero
Tel/fax: 383-0330
Tours can also be booked through the Mawamba Group
Tel: 223-2421; Fax: 222-5463
Email: mawamba@sol.racsa.co.cr
Website: www.crica.com/mawamba
A short hike from Tortuguero town, this 15-acre beachfront lodge has lush gardens with exotic birds and rustic, fan-cooled accommodation complete with rocking chairs. Swimming pool with jacuzzi, two family-style restaurants, bar, souvenir shop, and access to beach (though sea swimming is not recommended anywhere around Tortuguero). Boat ride and guided forest hike included in the rates. There is the possibility of arranging fishing or night turtle hikes. $$$

Pachiri Lodge
Tortuguero
Tel: 256-7080; Fax: 223-1119
Email: paccira@sol.racsa.co.cr
Website: www.pachiralodge.com
Located only five minutes away from Tortuguero National Park, the lodge offers 42 comfortable rooms, charmingly decorated with pastels and bamboo, built on stilts and connected by covered walkways. The lodge has a bar and restaurant and three nature trails, plus all the usual tours. $$$

Pacuare Nature Reserve
30 km (19 miles) northwest of Puerto Limón
Tel: 233-0451
Website: ww30w.rainforest.org.co.uk
An 800-hectare (1,976-acre) private reserve co-run by the Endangered Wildlife trust and Rainforest Concern which is open to ecotourists and volunteers who wish to particitpate in the turtle protection program. A beautiful lodge with only three bedrooms overlooks the beach and a freshwater lagoon that opens onto the main Tortuguero canal. The 6-km (3¾-mile) beach is one of the most important nesting sites for the leatherback turtle. Green turtles nest here from June through August. $$

Tortuga Lodge
Tortuguero
Tel: 710-6861
Or booked through its owner, Costa Rica Expeditions: www.expeditions.co.cr
Refurbished in 1997, Tortuga Lodge was the first lodge in the area and has won ecotourism awards for its support of the local community and its solar energy. The riverside verandah and pool are popular places to relax after a boat trip or hike. There are landscaped gardens as well as easy access to the rainforest, where howler monkeys and poison-arrow frogs may be spotted. $$$$

Puerto Viejo

El Pizote Lodge
Puerto Viejo
Tel: 221-0986; Fax: 255-1527/750-0088
Email: pizotelg@solracsa.co.cr
Website: www.hotels.co.cr./pizote.html
Recently renovated and surrounded by the jungle of Talamanca, the lodge is a 10-minute walk west from Puerto Viejo just across from the black beach. Some of the rooms and bungalows have private facilities. Restaurant, bar, and pool, plus cycles, snorkels and riding. $$

Selva Bananito Lodge
Between Puerto Limón and Cahuita
Tel: 253-8118
Email: conselva@solracsa.co.cr
Website: www.selvabananito.com
Opened in 1995, this secluded and comfort-

Top Left: Finca Rosa Blanca Country Inn
Right: great for wildlife watching

able family-run rainforest lodge and reserve is an excellent place to watch birds, climb trees, and rappel down waterfalls, take camping and riding trips or learn Spanish. $$

Shawanda Lodge
Puerto Viejo
Tel: 750-0018; Fax: 750-0037
Email: shawanda@sol.racsa.co.cr
Shawanda is designed like a primitive village nestled in more than two hectares (5 acres) of enormous ceiba trees and colorful tropical flowers. Each thatched bungalow has a romantic atmosphere, with traditional furnishings, large verandah, and unusual bathrooms. Good restaurant, and a 150-m (492-ft) private trail leads to the white sands of Playa Chiquita. $$$.

Villas del Caribe
Playa Chiquita, near Puerto Viejo
Tel: 233-2200; Fax: 221-2801
Email: info@villascaribe.net
Website: villascaribe.net
Delightful two-story beachfront units, each with kitchen, living area, terrace and barbecue. Set in a private 40-hectare (100-acre) reserve on a lovely beach. Easy to arrange snorkeling, riding, fishing, and diving. $$$

Guanacaste
Capitan Suizo
Playa Tamarindo
Tel: 653-0292; Fax: 683-0075
Email: capitainsuizo@ticonet.co.cr
Swiss-owned, this informal and elegant resort is close to the laid-back resort of Tamarindo, with access to the beach, free-form pool, and breeze-cooled dining room. Cool and spacious rooms made from local stone with hardwood floors and ethnic fabrics. Reservations

essential in high season as this is one of the most popular hotels in the region. $$$$

Hotel Las Torugas
Playa Grande
Tel/fax: 653-0458
Email: nela@cool.co.cr
Turtle-friendly hotel on a wide, long, and beautiful beach. Conservationist management. Good restaurant and pool, with excellent surfing directly in front of the hotel. $$$-$$$$

Melia Playa Conchal Beach & Golf Resort
Playa Conchal
Tel: 654-4123; Fax: 654-4181
Email:melia.playa.conchal@solmelia.es
The most luxurious and largest resort in Costa Rica, with golf course, tennis courts, and an enormous pool, yet not too obtrusive. It is also close to one of the best beaches in Guanacaste. $$$$

Nosara Retreat
Playa Nosara
Tel: 682-0071; Fax: 682-0072
Email: yogacr@solracsa.co.cr
Run by former directors of the famous Kripalu Center, this elegant hilltop villa is a unique retreat in Costa Rica, offering yoga, massage, and other holistic courses. Rates include daily yoga lessons. $$$$

El Ocotal Hotel
Playa Ocotal
Tel: 670-0321; Fax: 670-0083
Email: elocotal@sol.racsa.co.cr
Elegant and secluded hotel on a cliff with spectacular views of the ocean and beach. Rooms and bungalows, some with ocean views and Jacuzzis. Pool, tennis, fishing, sailing, and dive packages are available. $$$$

Punta Islita
Islita Beach, Nicoya
Tel: 231-6122; Fax: 296-0715
Email: ptaisl@solracsa.co.cr
Part of the Small Luxury Hotels of the World group, perched on a hill overlooking Playa Islita and the Pacific Ocean and one of Costa Rica's most romantic retreats. There are 20 deluxe bungalows and 12 suites with pri-

Left: Villas del Caribe
Top Right: El Ocotal Hotel

vate Jacuzzis. Superb open-air restaurant and pool overlooking the beach, which can be reached by shuttle or a 20-minute walk. Tennis, riding, and snorkeling available. $$$$

Central Pacific

Best Western
Jacó Beach
Tel: 643-1000; Fax: 643-3246
Website: bestwesterncostarica.com
Beachfront hotel with two pools, restaurants, good sports facilities including tennis and volleyball courts. Rooms are air-conditioned with private balconies. $$$

Costa Verde Hotel
Quepos
Toll free (US): 1-888 876 9373
E-mail: travel@informatica.co.cr
On the hillside outside Quepos, and only a few hundred yards/meters from the Manuel Antonio National Park. Comfortable rooms, restaurant, and cliff-side pools. $$$

Hotel Makanda-by-the-Sea
Quepos
Tel: 777-0442; Fax: 777-1032
Email: makanda@solracsa.co.cr
Located just off the main road between Quepos and Manuel Antonio Park, Makanda-by-the-Sea blends elegant architecture with a striking green backdrop in one of Costa Rica's richest natural settings. Secluded studios and villas, some with open-air living areas, plus infinity pool and Jacuzzi and access to a private beach only 10 minutes' walk away. $$$$

Si Como No
Quepos
Tel: 777-0777; Fax: 777-1093
Email: reservations@sicomono.com
An environmentally friendly resort, designed to blend in with its surroundings. Features include award-winning architectural design, pool with slide and swim-up bar, Jacuzzi and alfresco grill. Nature trails and free shuttle service to the nearby beach and national park. Highly recommended. $$$$

Villa Caletas
Punta Leona
Tel: 257-3653; Fax: 222-2059
Email: caletas@ticonet.cocr
Only minutes from the beaches of Herradura and Punta Leona, Villa Caletas is set high on a cliff with sweeping views of the Pacific. A colonial-style mansion with luxurious rooms, free-form infinity pool, fragrant gardens, terrace amphitheater and two open-air restaurant/bars. No TVs or phones in rooms. $$$$

The South

Albergue de Montaña Río Savegre
San Gerardo de Dota
Tel/Fax: 771-1732
Twenty-seven cabins with private showers and porches on the Chacón family farm in the cloud forests of San Gerardo. Rates include meals. $$–$$$

Casa Corcovado Jungle Lodge
Nr Playa San Josecito
Tel: 256-3181; Fax: 256-7409
Email: corocvodo@sol.racsa.co.cr
A 170-acre (69-hectare) private reserve bordering Corcovado National Park and a steep 10-minute climb from the beach. Individual breeze-cooled bungalows with ceiling fan and showers. Spring-fed pool, restaurant/bar with good forest views. $$$$

La Paloma Lodge
Drake Bay
Tel: 239-2801; Fax: 239-0954
Email: info@lapalomalodge.com
Pleasant, rustic bungalows and rooms built into the hillside overlooking the bay. Small pool to practice scuba diving. Good dive packages. Rates include meals. $$$$

Marenco Beach & Rainforest Lodge
Drake Bay
Tel: 258-1919; Fax: 255-1346
Email: info@marencolodge.com
Formerly a biological station now owned and operated by a Costa Rican family dedicated to protecting the rainforest, this 500-hectare (1,235-acre) reserve is set on a hill with views of the Pacific. Rustic cabins with private facilities, fans, and balconies. Naturalist-led hikes through Marenco's rainforest. Meals are included. $$$$.

The North

Arenal Observatory Lodge
La Fortuna area
Tel: 257-9489; Fax: 257-4220
Email: info@observatory.co.cr
Website: www.arenal-observatory.co.cr
Originally a research station and the only lodge within the park, this forest lodge is the best place for volcano-viewing. The more expensive rooms have picture windows with volcano views. Lots of observation decks and trails. Rates include meals. $$$$

Jungla y Senderos los Lagos
La Fortuna area
Tel: 479-9126; Fax: 479-8009
Pleasant white *cabinas* and great volcano views. Pool. Footpaths $$$

Montana de Fuego
Nr La Fortuna
Tel: 460-1220; Fax: 460-1455
Email: monfuego@solracasa.co.cr
Located at the base of Arenal Volcano with 24 wooden cabins, each with terrace and volcano view. Bar and restaurant. $$$

Monteverde Lodge
Monteverde
Tel: 257-0766; Fax: 257-1665
Booked as a package through Costa Rica Expeditions, website: www.expeditions.co.cr
Comfortable eco-friendly lodge 5km (3 miles) from Monteverde reserve to the southwest of Arena, and is the most comfortable base for exploring the cloudforest reserve. Spacious rooms with garden or forest views. Restaurant, bar, jacuzzi and tropical gardens. $$$$.

Rock River Lodge
Tilaran
Tel: 695-5644
Email: rokriver@solracsa.co.cr
Website: www.rockriver.mastermind.net
Small rustic lodge set above the lake offering excellent activities, including sailboarding, cycling, hiking, and riding. $$-$$$

Tabacon Lodge
La Fortuna
Tel: 256-1500
Fax: 221-3075
Email: tabacon@solracsa.co.cr
Website: www.tabacon.com
Part of the Tabacon Hot Springs Resort, this hotel has spacious rooms, some designed for guests with disabilities. Good volcano views, hot and cold pools and within walking distance of the springs. $$$$

HEALTH AND EMERGENCIES

Hygiene/General Health
The standard of Costa Rican health care ranks near to that in the USA, Canada, and other Western nations, especially in its private hospitals and clinics, which are often staffed by doctors trained in the USA and Europe.

Water in the Central Valley is drinkable, with few exceptions.

Medical/Dental Services
For emergency ambulance service in the Central Valley, tel: 911.

The following are excellent, private medical centers within the Central Valley: **Clinica Cristiano Jerusalem** (tel: 216-9191); **Catholic Clinic** (tel: 283-6166, fax: 283-6171, email: infoing@clinicacatolica.com); **Santa Rita Clinic** – maternity and gynecology (tel: 221-6433; fax 255 1248). Clinica Biblica (tel: 221-3922 or 800/911-0800) has a recommended emergency room. Outside the Central Valley, ask the manager of your hotel for details of medical centers.

For emergency dental care, contact Dr Arturo Acosta, tel: 228-9904. The *Tico Times* also lists English-speaking doctors and dentists.

Pharmacies

There are good-quality pharmacies throughout the Central Valley. Along the coast and in the mountains, however, there are very few.

CRIME/TROUBLE

Pickpocketing, chain- and watch-snatching, backpack-grabbing, and other such forms of theft have become a growing problem, especially in San José. You should feel more relaxed if you take a few common-sense precautions: don't carry valuables (jewelry, watches, cameras, sunglasses, electrical goods or extra cash) with you when you are out on the street; leave backpacks and purses at your hotel – carry only what you really need, and avoid walking on the streets at night, especially in areas away from the main thoroughfares.

When driving through the city, keep your windows rolled up; always lock your car and never leave unattended items inside. Do not assume that items in the trunk are safe. Do not leave belongings unattended at the beach.

COMMUNICATIONS AND NEWS

Mail

The central post office, is located in San José at Calle 2, Avenidas 1–3. Costa Rican postal services are generally slow and unreliable. Avoid receiving packages by mail while in Costa Rica. Outrageous duties are sometimes levied on incoming goods and you can spend days trying to get packages out of customs.

Telephones

Costa Rica has excellent telecommunications. For information and local directory assistance call 113 and for international information call 124. Phone cards are popular but certain cards work only with certain phones. E-mail is easily sent and received here, and there are several cybercafés in San José and the more popular tourism destinations.

Television

There are 45 TV channels received via cable, including about 25 channels in English.

Right: Costa Rica calling

Radio

Two radio stations in English include 107.5 FM, which plays classic rock and has news, as well as Radio Dos (99.5 FM), which has the news in English every other hour.

The Press

The English-language newspaper the *Tico Times* and a bilingual tourist magazine, *Costa Rica Today,* are published weekly, and both provide listings and general information. There are also a number of Spanish-language daily newspapers, including *La Nación, La República,* and *La Prensa Libre.*

USEFUL INFORMATION

Bookshops

Libreria Interacional

300m west of Taco Bell, behind San Pedro Mall. Tel 253-9553
Third floor of Multiplaza Shopping Center. Tel. 288-1138
English, French, German, and Italian books, plus Latin American authors in original and translation. Multilingual staff.

Libreria Central

Calle 30, Avenida Central at Plaza la Cultura Tel: 233-0713; fax: 223-1212
Latin American authors, both in original and translation, a section with Costa Rican literature as well as a variery of literature, in English. Multilingual staff.

The Bookshop
Calle 3 and Calle 3 bis Avenida 11
Well-known English bookshop with a small selection of English and Spanish books, friendly café and interesting local art gallery. Open Mon–Sat.

Yaohan's Newstand & Bookshop
Next to Yaohan's supermarket at the end of Paseo Colón, just off Calle 42.
Tel: 221-4664
Newspapers and magazines from around the world. Some best-selling paperbacks.

Mark Twain Library
Centro Cultural Costarricense/
Norteamericano
Los Yoses
Tel: 225-9433
About 200 yds/meters north of Centro la Mufla, near Los Yoses Automercado. English-language reference books, magazines, fiction, and non-fiction. Books can only be checked out by members, but anyone can use the library.

ATTRACTIONS

Museums
Costa Rican Art Museum
(Museo de Arte Costarricense)
Sabana Este at Paseo Colón
Tel: 222-7155
Permanent collection and hanging exhibits of paintings and sculpture by 19th- and 20th-century Costa Rican artists. The Cafe

Ruiseñor, on the patio, is expensive but a pleasant place for coffee and desserts. Open Tues–Sun 10am–4pm; admission free on Sun.

Gold Museum *(Museo de Oro)*
Below the Plaza de la Cultura
Calle 5, Avenida Central,
Tel: 223-0528
An impressive display of pre-Columbian gold jewelry and artifacts. Open Tues–Sun 10am–4.30pm.

Jade Museum *(Museo de Jade)*
11th Floor of the INS Building
11th floor, Calle 9, Avenida 7
Tel: 223-5800, ext. 2584
Extensive exhibits of pre-Columbian jade pieces, some of which have mysterious origins. Open Mon–Fri 9am–3pm.

National Museum *(Museo Nacional)*
Calle 17, Avenida Central (100yds/meters south of Parque Nacional)
Tel: 257-1433
Email: museonac@sol.racsa.co.cr
Website: www.museonacional.ulatina.ac.cr
Housed in the old Bellavista fortress, which still bears bullet marks from the Civil War. General overview of Costa Rica's history, with displays from the pre-Columbian and Colonial eras. Open Tues–Sun 8am–4.30pm; free admission for under 10s.

Natural History Center
Tortuguera
Tel: 233-7164.
Teaches about the wildlife of the area and features a Caribbean Conservation Visitors' Center. Books are sold at the museum: *The Windward Road* by Archie Carr, whose work is largely responsible for the founding of the park at Torruguera, is particularly recommended. This is also a good place to purchase laminated color plates of the birds of Costa Rica.

Gardens
Lankester Gardens
Apdo 1031-7050
Paraíso de Cartago
Tel: 551-9877
Offers more than 650 acres (243 hectares) of gardens and forest and over 800 species of

orchids. Best months to visit are Feb–Apr. Open daily, 8.30am–3.30pm. Tours available.

Arenal Botanical Gardens
Nuevo Arenal
Tel: 694-4273
Fax: 694-4086
Email: exoticseeds@hotmail.com
Botanical gardens founded in 1991. Over 1200 varieties of tropical plants and attractive trails, plus a butterfly farm. Open daily from 9am–4pm.

Tours
Café Britt's Coffee Tour
Heredia
Tel:260-2748; fax: 260-1456
Email: info@cafebritt.com
Coffee plantation where you can have a guided tour and learn about the history of coffee before a tasting session. A Café Britt bus picks up visitors from the main San José hotels – check with the manager or call the finca directly. You can also order from America by telephoning 1-800-462-7488.

WILDLIFE & ECOTOURISM

Only two-thirds the size of Scotland and representing only 0.03 percent of the world's surface, the tiny country of Costa Rica houses an incredible five percent of the global diversity in 12 different life forms.

In total there are about 13,000 plant species, including more than 1,000 species of orchids, 208 species of mammals, 850 species of birds, 220 types of reptiles, 163 varieties of amphibians, and 1,600 species of fresh- and salt-water fish. Costa Ricans have preserved this invaluable biodiversity in protected areas covering more than 25 percent of the national territory, and the country has often been cited as a model for conservation and the birthplace of ecotourism. As a result, thousands of visitors come to Costa Rica to enjoy its wildlife and scenery and there is a wide choice of activities and eco-lodges offering unique wildlife experiences.

However, the destination is in many ways a victim of its own success with many less scrupulous tour operators jumping on the ecotourism bandwagon, and investors and international chains trying to cash in by expanding mass tourism, which brings its own environmental problems. In addition, as admirable as Costa Rica's conservation initiatives may be, the country still faces the inevitable conflict between conservation and consumption and the threat of deforestation which leads to soil erosion.

As the debate continues between politicians, journalists, scientists, environmentalists, and various sectors of the tourism industry, many international charities and foundations have come to Costa Rica to assist the government in the protection of Costa Rica's invaluable natural wealth.

Many of the tour operators and travel companies recommended in this book have evolved a responsible attitude to business practices and sustainable tourism by using local guides and working with local communities in a sensitive way, controlling numbers to areas of natural beauty, discouraging unnatural interaction with the wildlife, and promoting small eco-lodges made from natural products rather than large resorts. The cost for these eco-friendly experiences may be higher than traditional tours and hotels but is outweighed by the benefit of supporting and conserving one of the planet's most important wildlife destinations.

Bird-Watching
Despite its small size, Costa Rica has roughly the same number of birds as the whole of North America and significantly more than Europe or Australia. Its incredible diversity, with over 850 species recorded, is partly explained by its many habitats, tropical location and its position on one of the world's great bird migration routes. An excellent field book is *A Guide to the Birds of Costa Rica* by F Gary Stiles and Alexander Skutch, published by Cornell University Press, 1989.

Top birding destinations are:
La Selva, near Puerto Viejo de Sarapiqui in the northern lowlands, where it is possible to see over 400 species in a variety of habitats. Contact La Selva Biological Research station through the Organisation for Tropical Studies, email: reservas@cro.ots.ac.cr
Tortuguero National Park (*see itinerary 6, page 36*), home to over 400 species of bird, including the Great Green macaw.

Cano Negro Wildlife Refuge *(see itinerary 15, page 56)* for waterfowl, including the Oliveaceous cormorant and Jabirú stork.

Carara Biological Reserve, near Jacó on the Central Pacific Coast is world-renowned for its Scarlet macaws.

Cerro de la Muerte *(see itinerary 11, page 48)*, in search of the Resplendent Quetzal.

Frog Watching

In Costa Rica there are around 160 species of amphibians, including poison-dart frogs, gaudy leaf frogs, and glass frogs. The best way to see frogs is to employ a guide who will know where the favorite hiding-places are. If, on your own, walk quietly and look at moist leaf litter, decomposing trees, and large-leaved plants such as philodendrons. Areas around streams, lakes, and marshes also tend to have large populations and they are easier to see during dawn and dusk. Frogs are more easily seen during the rainy season (May–Nov) when they lay and fertilize their eggs.

The top frog-watching destinations are:
La Selva Biological Station *(see bird-watching section, page 89)*
Tortuguero National Park
Rincón de la Vieja National Park
Carara Biological Reserve
Corocovado National Park.

Monkey Watching

Home to four different species of primates, Costa Rica is an excellent place to watch monkeys, The tiny squirrel monkey is the smallest and rarest species and exists in the south Pacific coastal rainforest, especially in Corcovado and Manuel Antonio Parks. The easily-spotted white-faced capuchin monkeys are widespread throughout the country and, like squirrel monkeys, travel in groups foraging for fruit and insects. Spider monkeys have long thin limbs and tail and rarely come down to the ground. They are most easily observed along the waterways of Tortuguero. Howler monkeys are named after their strange call and are often heard around dawn and dusk or when their territory is threatened. They can be found in Tortuguero and the dry forests of Guanacaste and the Nicoya Peninsula.

The best time to see monkeys is early morning and mid-afternoon, when family troops are on the move in search of food. You will probably hear them before seeing a movement in the canopy. Keep voices down, walk quietly and do not feed them.

Turtle Watching

There are few better places in the world than Costa Rica to observe sea turtles nesting. Home to the Green, Hawksbill, Olive Ridley, Leatherback and Loggerhead turtles. Costa Rica has since 1954 pioneered the conservation of turtles and has four major conservation sites.

As noise and light can confuse and frighten the turtles and cause them to return to the sea without laying eggs, it is vital to visit the nesting sites with a proper guide and obey the

strict regulations in place to protect these endangered species. Only one in 5,000 baby turtles will survive to reach adulthood and sea turtles are also threatened by hunting, polluted waters, and accidental capture by fishermen, but many former hunters have been re-educated as guides and there are foundations and eco-friendly operators working to increase the turtle population. For further information, contact the Caribbean Conservation Corporation at www.cccturtle.org.

Green turtles nest along the beaches of Tortuguero from July through October. Leather-backs nest along the Caribbean coast and at Las Baulas Marine National Park from Janurary through June. Hawksbills and Loggerheads nest along the Caribbean coast from November through April.

As many as 100,000 Olive Ridleys come to nest at the Ostional National Wildlife

Above: a humming bird hovers in the Manuel Antonio National Park

Refuge and leave more than 10 million eggs. This phenomenon is known as the *arribada* and occurs four to 10 times each year between July and November, usually before a new moon, although lesser numbers can be seen any time during the nesting season.

USEFUL ADDRESSES

Instituto Costarricense de Turismo (*Costa Rican Tourist Institute*),
Apdo 777–1000 Plaza de la Cultura at Calle 5 and Avenida Central, San José
Tel: (506) 223-1733; Fax: (506) 255-4997
Website: www.tourism-costarica.com
A toll-free number and bilingual operators are available to those calling from the USA, tel: (1 800) 343-6332.For details on Costa Rica's Travel Net, contact: TravelNet@centralamerica.com.

Fundacion de Parques Nacionales
(*National Parks Foundation*)
Calle 23, Avenida 15, San José
Tel: 257-2239 (8am–4pm)
The National Park Foundation administers the park system. Call them for information and permits. Most permits are also available at the park entrances.

The Tico Times
Tel: 222-8952; Fax: 233-6378
Email: ttimes@sol.racsa.co.cr

USEFUL TOUR OPERATORS

The following operators are all recommended for general activities in Costa Rica:

Costa Rica Expeditons
Tel: 257-0766
Website: www.expeditions.co.cr
Long-established and one of the most professional operators, which pioneered many ecotourism/adventure tours in Costa Rica.
Costa Rican Trails
Tel: 225-6000
Website: www.crtrails.co.cr
Small, friendly operator that specializes in flexible itineraries as well as adventure activities and self-drive and motor-bike tours.

Costa Rican Temptations
Tel: 220-4437
Website: www.crtinfo.com
Wide variety of tours and choice of accommodation across the country. Great service.
Horizontes
Tel: 222-2022
Wwebsite; www.horizontes.com
Well-known nature and adventure specialist that also caters for families and has been operating for many years.
Travel Excellence
Tel: 258-1046
Website: www.travelexcellence.com
Recommended operator for traditional and adventure/ecotourism activities.

FURTHER READING

Insight Guide: Costa Rica, Apa Publications, Singapore (1998). Detailed overview and insight into Costa Rican history, culture, and places to visit. Excellent essays and superb full-color photographs.
What Happen, A Folk History of Costa Rica's Talamanca Coast, by Paula Palmer, San José Publications in English, San José (1993). The history of Costa Rica's Caribbean coast, told in the words of the area's elders. Difficult to find in the bookstores; try ordering it from Apdo 7-1230, 1000 San José.
Costa Rica: A Traveler's Literary Companion, edited by Barbara Ras, Whereabouts Press, 3415 Geary Blvd. #619, San Francisco, CA 94118 (1994) An English translation of 26 stories by Costa Rican writers. Oscar Arias edition available on the Net.

USEFUL WEBSITES

Useful websites include:
www.tourism-costarica.com
www.tourism.co.cr
www.costaricanhotels.com
www.accommodations.co.cr
www.hotels.co.cr
www.ticotimes.co.cr (a useful source for listings and current affairs).
www.costaricamap.com is a good general tourism site with many maps of the country as well as general information and contact details.

practical information

The travel guides that replace a tour guide – now better than ever with more listings and a fresh new design

INSIGHT
Pocket Guides

Insight Pocket Guides pioneered a new approach to guidebooks, introducing the concept of the authors as "local hosts" who would provide readers with personal recommendations, just as they would give honest advice to a friend who came to stay. They also included a full-size pull-out map.

Now, to cope with the needs of the 21st century, new editions in this growing series are being given a new look to make them more practical to use, and restaurant and hotel listings have been greatly expanded.

INSIGHT GUIDES

The world's largest collection of visual travel guides

Now in association with

Discovery CHANNEL

ACKNOWLEDGEMENTS

All photography by **Glyn Genin** *except*

10 **Henry C Genthe**

Cover Design **Carlotta Junger**
Cartography **Maria Randall**

© APA Publications GmbH & Co. Verlag KG Singapore Branch, Singapore

credits

INDEX

index